MW01295767

SQL

*Comprehensive Beginners Guide to
SQL Programming with Exercises
and Case Studies*

© Copyright 2018 - All rights reserved.

The content contained within this book may not be reproduced, duplicated or transmitted without direct written permission from the author or the publisher.

Under no circumstances will any blame or legal responsibility be held against the publisher, or author, for any damages, reparation, or monetary loss due to the information contained within this book. Either directly or indirectly.

Legal Notice:

This book is copyright protected. This book is only for personal use. You cannot amend, distribute, sell, use, quote or paraphrase any part, or the content within this book, without the consent of the author or publisher.

Disclaimer Notice:

Please note the information contained within this document is for educational and entertainment purposes only. All effort has been executed to present accurate, up to date, and reliable, complete information. No warranties of any kind are declared or implied. Readers acknowledge that the author is not engaging in the rendering of legal, financial, medical or professional advice. The content within this book has been derived from various sources. Please consult a licensed professional before attempting any techniques outlined in this book.

By reading this document, the reader agrees that under no circumstances is the author responsible for any losses, direct or indirect, which are incurred as a result of the use of information contained within this document, including, but not limited to, — errors, omissions, or inaccuracies.

TABLE OF CONTENTS

Introduction

Thank you for choosing this book, 'SQL - Comprehensive Beginners Guide to SQL Programming with Exercises and Case Studies.'

In the last few decades, many programming languages have been developed, and there are only some that have stuck around. Some examples are C, which is a popular server development and operating system for embedded systems. When it comes to databases, the Structured Query Language (SQL) has been around since the 1970s.

You can use SQL to create, generate, manage and manipulate from relational databases. Most businesses prefer to use a relational database since it can store hundreds and thousands of rows of data. This is only when the database is designed well. SQL is the only database language that can be used to manage large databases. New languages cannot compete with SQL for this reason. Hence, it is important you learn to work with SQL, and also learn how you should manage data in SQL.

In this book, you will gather information about what SQL is and why it is important to learn SQL. This book also covers some of the basic commands that are used in SQL and explains how you can use those commands to manipulate information in tables and datasets. This book covers information on different data types, operators, and functions you can use to work with data and analyze data. There are many examples given across the book that will help you grasp a good understanding of what SQL is. Some exercises are also given in the book, which will help you practice some of the concepts you have learned in the book.

You should continue to practice if you want to master SQL. It is okay not to know what code to use when you start learning to code in a language. It is only when you practice that you will know where you should apply a specific operator or function.

Thank you for purchasing the book.

CHAPTER
ONE

The Basics of Getting Started with SQL

There are a variety of options to choose from when you want to learn a new language. Some of these languages will let you build your very own website and will also help you identify different ways in which you can reach out to your customers. These languages also help you convert potential customers into confirmed customers. Other languages allow you to develop applications and games for your phone. Some of these languages are advanced which makes it difficult for an amateur to start programming immediately. There are other languages like SQL that allow a business owner to keep track of the information they have without any challenges.

Companies often used the Database Management System or DBMS to store the different information about their company. This information includes customer data and sales data. DBMS is the first option that was introduced into the market, which made it easier to work with the data. Over the years, newer methods were developed which helped a business hold onto its information without any difficulty. The simplest DBMS systems designed now are more secure than the ones that were developed a few years ago.

Companies need to hold a lot of information, and some of the information will be personal like the customer's address, credit card information, date of birth, and so on. To maintain the safety of this information, the databases need to be secure. There should also be a way for people to connect the information to analyze the data. This was when the relational database management system was developed. This type of database is like the traditional database system but is more secure. It also uses more technology to ensure that the information is safe.

As a business owner, you will certainly want to look at different options and also pick what type of tool you want to use to manage the database. SQL is the perfect tool for this purpose since it is well designed and easy to use. This language was designed to manage businesses and provides multiple tools that will allow you to keep the information safe. In this book, we will look at what SQL is and why it is one of the best systems to use to analyze and protect your data.

What is SQL?

The Structured Query Language (SQL) is a programming language that makes it easier for a user to interact with different sets of data or tables in the database. These tables are always in the same system. The tool was developed in the 1970s, but it only gained popularity when IBM built a similar prototype and launched it in the market. Companies began to use this tool to analyze their businesses and also make some judgments about their business. Oracle was the language that IBM developed, and this tool is still being used by many businesses all over the world. Oracle and SQL are tools that help businesses keep the data safe and ensure that the data is always available for the owner to use. These languages make it easier for one to perform analysis because of the many tools that they provide the user.

How does it work with Databases?

When you work with SQL, you will learn how to look at the database. It means that you will look at groups of information. Organizations believe that they should store information in a way that it is accessible to their customers. This information should also help the business to analyze the workings of the business. When the business analyzes the information, it can use the findings to make informed decisions.

Regardless of which company you work for, you will use databases which are similar to SQL. For instance, the phone book is a classic example of a database. A phone book contains a lot of information about businesses and people. You will gather the following information about businesses and people – names, numbers and addresses. All this information can be found in one place. The database is also arranged in alphabetical order, to ensure that you can find the information easily. Unlike the phone book, the SQL database is not structured in the same way, but you can use it to extract all the information you need.

Relational Databases

The SQL tool is often used on relational databases. A relational database can segregate the data into tables and other types of logical units. These tables are interconnected in the database that allows you to make sense of the data based on the kind of information you are looking for. This is a good tool to use depending on what you want to do to or what information you are looking for. You should use the database to take the complex information and break it down into smaller pieces of information. It becomes easier for you to control and optimize the data depending on how you need it.

It is always good to use these types of databases since you can take in all the data and information you have about the business. These databases make it easier for you to use the data since you can break complex information into language that is easy for anybody to understand. The server will then look at the different parts and identify a way to make them fit together. You can also locate the information you are looking for quickly since you do not have to go through the entire database. You can also add some security to your data if you want to keep it safe from others.

Server and Client Technology

In the past, companies used mainframe computers which means that these machines held up a large system, and this system would be a great place to store and process information. The user can access the computer and interact with the mainframe. If you need the information to bring up the correct function, the terminals of the mainframe computer will rely on the information like the storage, memory and processor found in the system.

These systems do work well, and if you own a system that uses this method, there is nothing wrong with the system. There are however some better options that you can use since they are more efficient and will get the work done faster. This can only be found in a server and client system. These systems will use different processes to help you identify the results that you will need. The main computer, also called the server, is the one that the user can access. It means any user on your network can access these systems. They also need to ensure that they have the right credentials to access this information. Only when the users have the right information and are on the network, can they access the necessary information. These users can access this server from other servers or using a desktop computer. In this instance, the user is called the client, and it is extremely easy for the client and server to interact with the database.

Working with Internet-based database systems

The server and client technology are popular for many different businesses in the world. This works well for some companies, but some other things need to be taken care of because of the changes in technology. Many companies allow a user to access an online database from their system. Customers that have an account on the company website can use this database system to update or change the information. These customers can even pay online, check their orders, make their purchases and much more.

Since more companies are setting up their websites, you must ensure that you develop a good website that will give the customer a chance to check the information out. There may be times when you want to include some security information like passwords when a customer enters his or her personal information. Many companies will require a customer to do this, but these companies always give the information out for free.

This system is easy to handle, but there are a few different things that will happen behind the scenes to ensure that the queries work correctly. The customer can use the system and check this information out, but there is a lot of information which the server will need to piece together to ensure that the information will show up properly on the screen. This will also help to enhance the user's experience.

For example, you may notice that the web browser you currently use will use an SQL code or a program that is similar to it. This program is to figure out what type of data the user hopes to see. The browser will use the SQL interface to reach the database once the customer has put in the information they are looking for. The SQL system will look at the query and will then bring the information back onto the website. This information will show up on the web browser, and only the right information will show up on the screen if the system works properly.

Benefits of Working with SQL

Now that you know about the different database systems that you can work with, let us learn about the advantages of using the Structured Query Language. In addition to a variety of coding languages, you also have some database languages, and each of these languages is different when compared to the other. You may also wonder why you should use SQL over other languages. Therefore, it is important that you know the benefits of SQL.

High speed

You should use the SQL system if you want to go through volumes of information quickly. The SQL system can find you a lot of information within a few seconds. You will also find the information that you need. If you work with volumes of data, you should use SQL since it is one of the most efficient options.

Standards that are well defined

If you want to ensure that your database is secure and strong, you should use SQL since it is constantly updated. These updates help to keep the SQL system strong. Other database tools will not have the same standards like SQL, which will affect your analyses. The features in other databases will also make it difficult for you to store all the necessary information.

You Do Not Need to Code

You do not need to code to use the SQL tool. All you need to do is remember a few syntaxes, which we will cover in the later chapters of the book. You, however, do not have to master coding in SQL if you want to use it to perform any analyses on some data.

Object-oriented DBMS

Since you will use a database management system when you work with SQL, it makes it easier for you to find all the information you need, store that information and perform the necessary analysis to make informed decisions.

You Can Earn A Lot of Money

You always want to earn more when you work for an organization. You can certainly get a better salary if you know how to use SQL. You can do this by either nurturing your programming skills in SQL or by learning how to maintain a system and keep it running effectively and efficiently. You can also work as an SQL analyst and provide information and insights for a business; it will help the seniors make better decisions. This will help to maximize the profits for any business.

All Types of Technology Uses SQL

Most businesses use database tools and technologies like MySQL, Microsoft SQL Server, and PostgreSQL. You should also remember that most people use SQL at some point in their lives. If you are not aware, you also use SQL on your smartphone.

Employers Look for SQL Skills

Most employers actively look for people who know how to use SQL. Yes, an employer is willing to pay you more, but he or she also is aware of the benefits of hiring an individual who is skilled at using SQL. If you want to move jobs or change your area of work, you should learn how to code in SQL. You will be one of the most sought-after candidate for the position

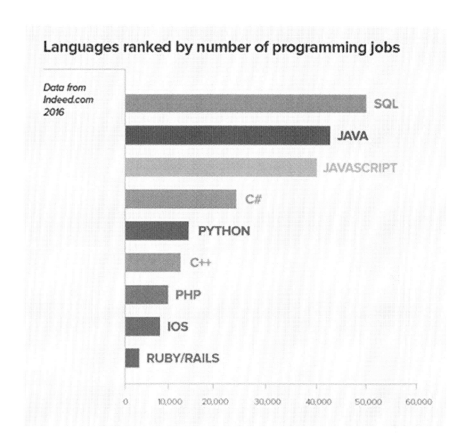

Languages ranked by number of programming jobs

Data from Indeed.com 2016

SQL
JAVA
JAVASCRIPT
C#
PYTHON
C++
PHP
IOS
RUBY/RAILS

0   10,000   20,000   30,000   40,000   50,000   60,000

You Always Obtain an Answer

You should think about the different questions you have about the data. You may want to know more about the sales from last year. Were your customers satisfied with your product? Have your expenses reduced since last year? You can answer all these questions using SQL. When you identify the database that provides this information, you can use SQL to explore that data to answer your questions. SQL allows you to analyze data in different ways. You do not have to rely only on simple reports or even contact your employers to obtain data. You can become an independent employee when you use SQL.

The Size of a File Never limits you

Have you ever had a problem where a spreadsheet has crashed because you have hundreds or thousands of rows filled with data? You can opt for a relational database to save the data since these databases can save millions of rows and columns of data with ease. SQL will allow you to perform different operations on the data and use that information to make decisions. It is true that MS Excel is a great tool to use, but this tool is not equipped to perform multiple operations on millions of rows of data. You should try to use a relational database to store the information and use SQL to perform any analysis on the data.

Reports Are Easy to Create

You can save SQL queries easily and re-use them whenever necessary. You can also make changes to the query any time you want to. You can also use comments in the SQL code that makes it easier for you and for anybody else to understand the query. If you work only on spreadsheets, you will need to include long multi-step processes. You will first need to import the data into excel from a report, tabulate it, sort it, and then filter or use some values depending on your need.

If you use SQL, you only need to write the code once, save that code and re-open it whenever you need to produce a report. You will save many hours and days. These are some of the benefits you can enjoy when you work with SQL. Some people claim that the SQL interface is slightly hard to use, and there are some features that you may need to purchase from a third party. In simple words, SQL has many features that make it easy for one to use the language. Since this language has multiple benefits, it is one of the best languages to use to perform analyses on different data sets that you collect for your business.

You may say that it is hype when I ask you to learn SQL, but you should remember that numbers never lie. SQL is an invaluable tool that many employers desire. Since most of the information is now digital, you have more data available to you. All this information is either stored in a database or a data warehouse. If you want to manage these databases or warehouses, you need to learn SQL. If you read a business journal, you will see that most businesses are looking for business intelligence analysts. If an organization wants to do more with the data it has, it should have individuals who know how to access and analyze data. You can do this through SQL.

TWO

Basic SQL Commands

Now that we know a bit more about SQL and some of the commands that one can use when they use SQL, it is time to learn a few of the commands that you would need to use to get this system to work. Luckily, SQL is easy to learn, and you won't have a lot of different commands in order to bring up the information that you want. In this chapter, we are going to spend some time learning some of these commands as well as separating the commands into the six different categories that are the best for them. These six categories include:

Data Definition Language

This one is also known as the DDL, and it is one of the aspects that is inside of your SQL program that is in charge of allowing you to generate objects into the database before arranging them the way that you enjoy the best. For example, this is the aspect of the system that you will use when you would like to make changes, such as adding or deleting objects, out of the table. There are a few different commands that you would be able to use for this including:

- Drop index

- Drop view

- Create index

- Alter index

- Alter table

- Drop table

- Create table

Data Manipulation Language

This is the one that is often called DML inside of your SQL program. This is also the one that you are going to use when you would like to do some modifications to the objects inside the database. This is a good method to use if you want to update an object, delete some of the objects, or makes sure that the right information is inserted into the database. This is going to give more freedom to the user whenever they want to go through all their information and add in something new that helps out the database.

Data Query Language

When you are working in DQL, you are working with what many consider a really powerful aspect of what they are able to do with SQL, especially when you are working on a database system that is considered more modern. There is just one command that is needed in order to work with the DQL part, and this command is the "Select" command. You are able to use this command in various ways including using it to run queries when you are inside of a relational database. If you were interested in getting results that are more detailed, you would need to use the Select command through DQL to make this happen.

Data Control Language

The DCL is another component of SQL that you should learn to use, and it is the commands that the user works with any time that they want to control who is allowed to get on the database. If you are dealing with personal information like credit card information, it is a good idea to have some limitations on who can get onto the system and get the information. This DCL command is used to help generate the objects that are related to who can access the information in the database, including who will be able to distribute the information. There are a few commands that are helpful when you are working on DCL including:

- Create synonym

- Grand

- Alter password

- Revoke

Data Administration Commands

When it comes to some of the commands that you can use inside SQL, you can also use them in order to audit or analyze the operation that is inside of the database. There are some instances where you will be able to access the performance of the database overall with the help of some of these commands. If you would like to fix something that is causing issues on the system or you would like to get rid of some of the bugs on the system, these are the commands that you are going to need to work with. While there are some options that you can choose from with these commands, the two most popular options include:

- Stop audit
- Start audit

One of the things that you need to remember when working with SQL is that data administration and database administration are going to be two different ideas inside the system. For example, database administration is going to be the part that will manage all your database, including the different commands that you are setting up in SQL and they will also be more specific to the implementation that is done in SQL.

Transactional Control Commands

If you are trying to manage and keep track of some of the transactions that are going on with your database with you and the customer, the transactional control commands are the right ones to use. If you are a company that uses their website in order to sell products online, the transactional control commands are going to help make sure that you can keep all of this in line. There are several things that you will be able to use these transactional control commands for, including:

Commit

This is the command that you will need to use in order to save information that relates to the different transactions that are inside your database.

Savepoint

This is the command that you will be able to use in order to generate different points inside the group of transactions. This is also the one that you can use at the same time as the Rollback Command.

Rollback

This command is the one that you will use whenever you are looking through the database, and you would like to undo at least one of the transactions inside.

Set transaction

This command is the one that you can use any time that you are trying to take the transactions in your database and give them names. You will often use this one whenever you are trying to label things for a bit more organization.

All six of these types are going to be important based on the results that you would like to get out of your search. Each of these will be explored a bit more as we go through this guidebook so that you understand better how to use them, when to use them, and how to divide up the information in the proper way to avoid issues and to keep your database nice and organized with the help of the SQL language.

THREE

Data Types That You
Can Use Inside of SQL

The next thing that we are going to look at is the different data types that you are able to use when working with SQL and creating your new code. These are going to vary based on what you are trying to do within the database as well as the different items that you are trying to offer or sell to the customer. The data types that are most commonly found inside of SQL are going to be the attributes that will go with the information that is inside and then these specific characteristics are going to be placed into a table so that you are able to retrieve and read them easily.

A good example of this is when you require that a field is only able to hold on to numeric values. You would be able to use SQL to set it up so that the user is not able to place anything outside of a number within the database, or at least in that particular cell of the table. If you want the person to only put their credit card number or their phone number, this would be a useful tool to ensure that they aren't accidentally putting something else there. By assigning the right kinds of data to the different fields inside of the database, you are ensuring that there are fewer errors in the entry of data on the side of the customer.

One thing that you should remember when you are working with SQL is that every version is going to be a bit different and you will need to use some different choices when it comes to the types of data that you are using. You will need to check out the rules of your version of SQL to make sure that it is all staying in order. For most cases, you will need to use the data points that are specific to your version so that the database is set up better.

The different data types that SQL supports depends on the history of the tool you are using. The SQL: 2003 specification recognizes only five predefined general types:

- Numerics
- Boolean
- Datetimes
- Strings
- Intervals

There will be more than one subtype within each of these types and we will cover them in detail in the next few chapters. In addition to the built-in, predefined types, SQL: 2003 supports collection types, constructed types, and user-defined types.

If you use an SQL implementation that supports one or more data types that the SQL: 2003 specification doesn't describe, you can keep your database more portable by avoiding these undescribed data types. Before you decide to create and use a user-defined data type, make sure that any DBMS you may want to port to in the future also supports user-defined types.

Characters Fixed in Length

So now we are going to spend some time looking at the different data types. The first one that we will look at is the fixed length characters. If you are working with constant characters or even strings that can stay the same all the time, you need to make sure that they are saved properly, which means you must save them as a fixed length data type. The typical data type that you will use when we are working with these options is:

CHARACTER (n)

In this situation, the "n" that is inside the parenthesis is going to be the maximum length, or the assigned length, that you would allow the field to be. For example, this could be the phone number of the customer. You would not want them to put in a number that is more than ten characters long, so you would set your "n" to be 10. Now, there are some variations on how you do this. Let's say that for the name you will set the length just to be 20. If someone has a small name, like Sam, they are able to use it in here, but they would not be able to go above the 20-character limit; it can always be smaller, though.

There are also some implementations of the SQL language that will use the "CHAR" data type just so that you are able to save information that is going to be a fixed length. It is a good idea to work with this kind of data type when you would like to work with information that is alphanumeric. For example, you would like to set up a part that has the user place in their state name, but you would like them to use the abbreviation rather than the whole name of the state. You would then be able to set the character limit to just be two parts so that everyone knows how to put things in.

When you work inside this particular data type, your user will not be adding information that is longer than whatever you have set. Let's say that they live in South Dakota, but if you set it up so that they are only allowed to put in two characters for the name of the state, they would need to put in SD rather than South Dakota.

There are many places where you are able to limit the amount of characters that you would like to use, but when it comes to the username and password that the user picks, you should not use the fixed length data types. The user will need to make up the username and password credentials that work for them and some people will pick a much longer one to make it safe.

Variable Characters

Another option that you can work with is the variable characters. Instead of limiting the user to how many characters they are able to use inside of this, they will be able to pick the length. This one works well for things like names (which can be varying lengths) as well as passwords and usernames to make them more unique. If you would like to use this option, the following notation can help you out:

CHARACTER VARYING (n)

In this option, you are going to use the "n" to be the number that identifies the assigned, or the maximum length, of your field. You will be able to pick from several different types to use when you want to work with these variable characters including VARCHAR, ANSI, and VARCHAR2.

For this data type, there isn't going to be a requirement that has to be met when it comes to filling out the spaces that your user can work with. If the length that you assigned here is 15 characters, the user is able to add in less if they would like and there wouldn't be issues with what they are doing.

Any time that you want to work with character strings that are considered variables, you will want to make sure that you are using the data type of varying as much as possible. This will help you to maximize the amount of space that is inside of your database, and you will be able to ensure that the user is able to put in their right information without a lot of issues in the process.

Numeric Values

It is also possible for you to work with numeric values that are in SQL. These values are the ones that are stored right inside your field as a number rather than a letter. These values are going to go by a different name, basically depending on the type that you are working with. There are several types of these numerical values that you can work with including:

- DECIMAL(p, s)

- REAL(s)

- BIT(n)

- FLOAT(p)

- INTEGER

- DOUBLE PRECISION(P)

- BIT VARYING(n)

Literal Strings

The next part of the data that you can work with is known as the literal strings. These are the series of characters, including things like phone numbers and names, which will be specified by the program user or the database. For the most part, you will find that these strings are going to have a lot of data that is similar in the characteristics.

When you work with these literal strings, you are going to have some trouble specifying the type of data that is going to be used. Rather, you are in charge of specifying the type of string that you want to use to make this work. It is good to note that when you work on these kinds of strings, especially the kinds that are alphanumeric, you will need to make sure that you are adding in some quotes around the words. You can choose between the double or single quotes on here, just make sure that you are using the same one on both parts.

Boolean Values

The Boolean values are important because they are going to help you out quite a bit when you are working inside of the SQL program. When you are working on these kinds of values, there are going to be three different values that you can work with null, false, or true. You will also find when using the Boolean values that you are looking into comparing the various units of data. It is going to take the information that you are working on and compare; you will get the answers that are above. For example, if you are working in SQL, you can specify the parameters of a search, and all the conditions that come back will either be null, false, or true depending on what you are trying to compare.

When you are working on the Boolean values, it is only going to give you the results when the answer is going to be true. If this answer is going to false or null, the data is not going to be retrieved for the customer or for you. If you do get a value that is true, you will be able to see all the information that is true. A good example of this is when the user does a search through your database. If the keywords of the products match with what the user is looking for, these true answers are going to show up.

As an online store, using the Boolean values is going to be one of your best assets. It is going to ensure that you are able to get the results that you or the user needs when doing a search. It is going to make sure that the right products come up based on the keywords that your customer is using and that all the items that don't match up stay away. You will be able to use these Boolean expressions in order to set your system up to retrieve the information that your customer is really looking for. Don't worry if this sounds complex; the SQL system is going to be able to help you get this done in a simple manner so that your customers find the things that they want without having to worry or fight with the website.

There are many different applications where you will be able to use some of the Boolean expressions in SQL, but as a beginner, this is probably the method that you will use the most often. You are also able to use it when you want to look through your database and find specific answers to questions, or when you are looking through the store or program and want to find specific information. When you add some of this information into tables in SQL, you are able to speed this process up more than ever before.

As you can see through this chapter, there are many data types that you will be able to work with inside of SQL in order to make your searches and program easier to use. Each data type is going to work differently so that you can get the right results and more that you need.

In addition to the commands, several other words have a special significance within SQL. These words, along with the commands, are reserved for specific uses, so you can't use them as variable names or in any other way that differs from their intended use. You can easily see why tables, columns, and variables should not be given names that appear on the reserved word list. Imagine the confusion that a statement such as the following would cause:

SELECT SELECT FROM SELECT WHERE SELECT = WHERE;

FOUR

An Introduction
to Numeric Data Types

Absolute Numerics

The numeric data type will allow you to express every value you enter as a number. The following data types fall into this category:

- Integer

- Bigint

- Smallint

- Numeric

- Decimal

Integer Data Type

The integer data type does not have a fractional part, and the precision of the number solely depends on the implementation of SQL. You must remember that the database developer does not specify the precision. The precision of a number is defined as the maximum number of digits that you can enter for a number.

Smallint Data Type

Smallint is a type of integer, and the precision of this data type in a specific implementation cannot be greater than the precision of the integer in the same implementation. The implementation of the 370 computers/IBM system represent the INTEGER and SMALLINT data types using a 32-bit and 16-bit binary numbers. In most database tools, the INTEGER and SMALLINT data types are the same data type.

If you want a database column only to hold integer data, the range of values in your column will never exceed the length of the SMALLINT data type. It is a good idea to opt for the SMALLINT data type since it helps the database management system conserve space.

Bigint Data Type

The BIGINT data type was first added in the 2003 version of SQL. This is also an integer data type, and this data type is defined as a type with a precision greater than the INTEGER type. Since the BIGINT data type does not depend on the implementation, the SQL interface will not define an exact precision.

Numeric Data Type

You can include a fractional component to the numeric data type apart from the integer component. You can also specify the scale and precision of the NUMERIC data type. The scale of the number in this data type is the number of digits that can be included after the decimal point. The scale can never be negative or larger than the precision.

If you declare that a variable will take a numeric data type, the SQL implementation will give you the exact scale and precision. You can specify the numeric data type and let SQL use the default scale and precision. Alternatively, you can use NUMERIC (p) and only specify the precision and use the NUMERIC (p,s) if you want to specify both the precision and scale. The parameters p and s will be replaced by the values.

For example, if the precision for the numeric data type is 12 and the scale is 6, a column in the database with the numeric data type can only hold numbers up to 999999.999999. If you specify the data type NUMERIC (10) for any column, the column can only hold a maximum of 9999.999999. The parameter (10) will specify the number of digits that you can include in a number. If you specify the data type NUMERIC (10,2), the column will still hold numbers with ten digits; however, two digits will be to the right side of the decimal point.

The numeric data type is used for values like 595.72. This value has a limit of 5, which is also called the precision, and a scale of 2. The scale indicates the number of digits that you can enter on the right side of the decimal point. You can declare the data type as NUMERIC (5,2).

Decimal Data Type

The DECIMAL data type is similar to the numeric data type. It can also have a fractional component, and you can specify the scale and precision. The difference is that the precision of the query is always greater than when you use the decimal data type instead of the numeric data type. The SQL tool will use a default value as it does with a numeric data type if you do not specify the precision or scale.

If you specify an item as NUMERIC (5,2), this number can never be greater than 999.99. If you specify the data type as DECIMAL (5,2), you can enter values up to the number 999.99. If the system allows you to use larger values, the DBMS will not reject those values.

You can opt for the DECIMAL or NUMERIC data type if you have some fractional numbers in your data. You should only use INTEGER, SMALLINT, and BIGINT if the data you use only consists of whole numbers. You should use the numeric data type if you want to improve portability. If you define a numeric data type as NUMERIC (5,2), the SQL interface will hold the same range of values on every system.

Approximate Numerics

Some quantities have a large range of values. This means that a computer cannot represent all the values in the numbers in the exact same order. The examples of register sizes are 32 bits, 64 bits or 128 bits. In most cases, there is no need to have an exact value, since a close approximation is always acceptable. There are three types of approximation that can handle this type of data.

Real Data Type

The REAL data type will give you a single-precision floating point numbers, and this precision number is dependent on the implementation. The hardware you use will determine the precision of this value. If you use a 64-bit machine, the system will give you more precision when compared to a 32-bit machine.

A floating-point number is one that includes a decimal point. The decimal point will appear in different parts in the number depending on what the value of the number is. Some examples are 3.14. 3.4566 and 3.55.

Double Precision Data Type

The precision of the double precision data type depends on the implementation. This data type will return a double-precision floating-point number. The meaning of the world DOUBLE depends solely on the implementation. Only scientific users use the double precision data type. Different scientific disciplines require different levels of precision, and there are some SQL implementations which will cater to your needs.

In some systems, the DOUBLE precision type has twice the capacity of REAL data type for both the exponent and mantissa. You never gain any benefit by representing a number that is fairly close to a number with an approximate numeric data type. You can use exact numeric data types as well since they are exact numbers.

If you use the SQL 2003 version, you do not have to establish or arbitrate the meaning of DOUBLE PRECISION. The only rule here is that the DOUBLE PRECISION number should always be greater than that of a REAL number. This constraint is weak but is possibly one of the most common differences you will encounter in hardware.

Float Data Type

You should use the FLOAT data type if you think that the database will move to a different hardware platform. You should specify the precision of the data type by including the data type size in parentheses. For example, you can specify this data type as follows: FLOAT (5). Your system will use single-precision arithmetic operations if the hardware you use supports single-precision circuitry. If you specify a precision that needs to use double-precision arithmetic, the system will always use a double-precision arithmetic method.

You should use the FLOAT data type instead of the DOUBLE PRECISION or REAL data type since it makes it easier for you to port your databases to other hardware. This is because the FLOAT data type will enable you to specify the exact precision. For both DOUBLE and REAL, the precision is dependent on the hardware.

If you are unsure of whether you should use the exact numeric data type or the approximate numeric data type, you should always use the exact numeric data type. It is because the exact data type does not use too much of the resources and always gives you the exact results instead of the approximate results. You can use the approximate data type if you are certain of the fact that your data is large enough.

Operators in SQL

There are different operators that you can use in SQL to perform different types of operations on the operands. These operators are addition (+), subtraction (-), multiplication (*) and division (/). You can also perform some operations on dates using the addition and subtraction operators.

Syntax

The syntax is as follows:

SELECT <Expression>[arithmetic operator]<expression>...

FROM [table_name]

WHERE [expression];

In the syntax above, the expression is made up of a single constant, variable scalar function or column name. This can also be used to compare the values of one variable against another variable.

FIVE

An Introduction to Character Strings

You can store a variety of information in a database including sounds, animations and graphic images. This chapter covers some information about the different character data types that you can use in SQL, and these are used as often as the numeric data types.

There are three main character data types – Fixed character data (CHAR or CHARACTER), varying character data type (VARCHAR or CHARACTER VARYING) and character large object data (CLOB or CHARACTER LARGE OBJECT). There are three variants of these character types – NATIONAL CHARACTER, NATIONAL CHARACTER VARYING and NATIONAL CHARACTER LARGE OBJECT.

Character Data Type

If you define the data type for any column as either CHAR or Character, you can also specify the number of characters that the column can hold by using the CHARACTER (x) function. In this function, the variable x defines the number of characters that you can add in the column. If you specify the data type as CHARACTER (16), you can only enter a maximum of 16 characters in the column. If you do not specify any argument, SQL will assume that you can only enter a character with a field length of one. If you enter any data into the CHARACTER field with fewer characters when compared to the specified number, SQL will fill the remaining space using blanks.

Character Varying Data Type

The CHARACTER VARYING data type will allow you to enter data in a column with different lengths, but you must ensure that SQL does not fill the empty character spaces using blanks. This data type will also enable you to store only the number of characters that you enter. There is no default value that exists in SQL for this data type. You can use the form VARCHAR (x) and CHARACTER VARYING (x) if you want to specify this data type. The x in the parentheses is the maximum number of characters that you can enter.

Character Large Object Data Type

It was only in the SQL 1999 version that the CHARACTER LARGE OBJECT (CLOB) was introduced. This data type is a huge character string that is very large for the character data type. The CLOBs have the same attributes as ordinary character strings, but there are many restrictions on how you can use this data type. You can use a CLOB in a FOREIGN KEY, a UNIQUE predicate and a PRIMARY KEY. You cannot use it for any comparison operations or functions. It is because of their large sizes that most applications do not transfer the CLOBS from one database to another. You can use the CLOB locator to manipulate any CLOB data. This is a parameter whose value will identify with a large character object.

35

National Character, National Character Varying and National Character Large Object Data Type

Every language has different characters. For instance, the English and German languages differ in the sense that some characters in English will not be present in German, and vice versa. For instance, if you use an English character set as your default settings in your system, you can use the alternate character sets because the NATIONAL CHARACTER VARYING, NATIONAL CHARACTER LARGE OBJECT and NATIONAL CHARACTER data types function in the same way as the CHARACTER VARYING, CHARACTER LARGE OBJECT and CHARACTER data types. You must remember that the character set that you specify is very different from a default character set. You can, however, use different character sets if you want. Let us look at the following examples of using multiple character sets:

CREATE TABLE XLATE

   (

LANGUAGE_1 CHARACTER (40),

LANGUAGE_2 CHARACTER VARYING (40) CHARACTER SET GREEK,

LANGUAGE_3 NATIONAL CHARACTER (40),

LANGUAGE_4 CHARACTER (40)

CHARACTER SET KANJI

) ;

The column Language_1 will contain the characters that are included in the default character set. The Language_3 will only contain the characters in the national character set, the Language_4 column will only have Kanji characters, and the Language_2 column will only contain Greek characters.

Booleans

The Boolean data type only returns true or false values. If you use a Boolean operator and compare that data type to an unknown value or a null value, the result will always be the unknown or null value.

CHAPTER
SIX

An Introduction to Datetimes

There are five standard data types in the 2003 version of SQL, which deal with time and dates. These types are all called the datetimes or datetime data types. You should also consider the overlap that exists between these data types, so it is important that you learn how to implement these data types.

An implementation that does not fully support these data types for all dates and times will experience problems if you want to switch from one implementation to another. If you are unsure of how to migrate between the data types, you should check the source and the destination implementation that will represent dates and times.

Date Data Type

This data type will store the year, day and month values of a date. The length of this data type is four, two and two for the year, month and day respectively. You can use this data type to represent a date between 0001 and 9999. The data type has ten positions, and the data can be entered in the following format – 1957-06-10. Since SQL represents the four digits in the year, it did not face the problems that other database languages faced when the year 2000 was included.

Time without Time Zone Data Type

The time without time zone data type will store every value of time including the hour, minute and second. The hours and minutes will be represented by whole numbers, but the second's value can be a single, double or fractional value. This data type will, therefore, represent a time of 20 minutes and 45.366 seconds past 8 a.m. in the following format – 08:20:45.366.

The precision of every fractional data type solely depends on the implementation but can hold six digits. The time without time zone value can take up only eight positions including the colons. This can only happen if you do not include a fractional part. The data type will hold nine positions if you include a fractional digit. You can either use the TIME WITHOUT TIME ZONE data type as TIME where you do not include fractional digits or use the TIME WITHOUT TIME ZONE (p) where you can define the number of digits you want to have to the right of the decimal point. The example in the previous paragraph will represent the data type TIME WITHOUT TIME ZONE (3).

Timestamp without Time Zone Data Type

The TIMESTAMP WITHOUT TIME ZONE data type will include both the date and time information. This data type has the same lengths and restrictions as the TIME WITHOUT TIME ZONE and DATE data types. There is however one difference – the fractional part of the component of the TIMESTAMP WITHOUT TIME ZONE can only hold six digits. It cannot include a zero. If there are no fractional digits in the date, the length of the TIMESTAMP WITHOUT TIME ZONE has nineteen positions where ten positions are for the date; one space is used as a separator and the eight positions for the time. If there are any fractional digits in the value, the length of the data type will be twenty digits, including the fractional digits. The twentieth position of the type is only for the decimal point. You can specify the field as the TIMESTAMP WITHOUT TIME ZONE using either TIMESTAMP WITHOUT TIME ZONE (p) and TIMESTAMP WITHOUT TIME ZONE. Here the value of p determines the number of fractional positions, and this value cannot be negative. The implementation of the data type will determine the maximum value that any value can take.

Time with Time Zone Data Type

This data type is like the Time Without Time Zone data type with the exception that the former data type will add information about the offset from the Greenwich Mean Time or GMT. The value of this offset can range from anywhere between -12:59 or +13:00. The additional information will take six more positions after the time. The additional information is always followed by a hyphen which is used as a separator. This separator is followed by a plus or minus sign and the offset in hours and minutes which take up two digits each. There will be a colon in between hours and minutes. If there is no fractional part in the time with time zone value, the data type is fourteen positions long. If you do specify the fractional part, then the field length is fifteen positions in length and an additional number of digits for the fractional portion of the data type.

Timestamp with Time Zone Data Type

The Timestamp with Time Zone data type is the same as the timestamp without time zone data type. The only exception is that this data type includes the offset information from universal time. This additional information will take up more than six-digit positions following the timestamp. If you include the time zone data with no fractional part, it will include twenty-five positions. If you include the time zone data with a fractional section, you can use twenty-six positions and the number of fractional digits for the parts of the data type that includes a fractional part.

SEVEN

An Introduction to Intervals

The interval data type is similar to the date time data type in SQL. The interval is calculated as the difference between two date time numbers or values. In most applications, you always need to be able to calculate the interval between two times or dates. You can use two types of interval data types in SQL namely the daytime interval and year-month interval. The number of years and months between two dates is called the year-month interval, and the number of days, minutes, hours and seconds between two events or instances in a specific period is called the daytime interval. You cannot combine the calculations that involve a daytime interval with a year-month interval since months vary in length (28, 29, 30 and 31 days).

Row Type

The ROW data type was introduced in the 1999 version of SQL and is a slightly difficult data type to understand. You probably may not use it if you are a beginner. People were able to work with SQL just fine before this data type was introduced.

A notable thing about this data type is that it does not follow the rules of normalization. E.F. Codd defined normalization theory when the relational databases were first built. A table in the normal form can never have multiple values in a table row. Every field can only contain one value. The ROW data type allows you to store lots of information in one field or a single row in a table. This means that you can nest information within a row using this data type.

The following SQL statement shows how you can use the ROW data type to store a person's personal information:

CREATE ROW TYPE addr_typ

(

Street   CHARACTER VARYING (25)

City   CHARACTER VARYING (20)

State   CHARACTER (2)

PostalCode   CHARACTER VARYING (9)

) ;

After it's defined, the new ROW type can be used in a table definition:

CREATE TABLE CUSTOMER (

CustID   INTEGER   PRIMARY KEY,

LastName   CHARACTER VARYING (25),

FirstName   CHARACTER VARYING (20),

Address   addr_typ Phone

CHARACTER VARYING (15)

) ;

The plus here is that if you are maintaining address information for multiple entities — such as customers, vendors, employees, and stockholders — you only have to define the details of the address specification once, in the ROW type definition.

Collection Types

It was only in the year 1999 that people could violate the normal form in SQL since they could enter a collection of objects in a field instead of just one. The ARRAY data type was introduced in 1999 and the MULTISET data type was introduced in 2003.

You can compare these collections to each other if they are of the same data type. This is because the variables in an array follow an element order, and you can compare corresponding elements in another array. A multiset does not follow a defined element order, but you can compare the values if enumeration exists for every multiset that you are comparing. In this instance, you can pair the enumerations to compare them.

Array Type

Unlike the row data type, the array data type violates the first normal form. The ARRAY type is not a data type like CHARACTER or NUMERIC but is a collection data type. The Array type allows a field to have multiple values of the same data type. Let us assume that your organization wants to contact customers regardless of whether they are on the road, at home or at work. You can maintain multiple telephone numbers for your customers by declaring an array. The syntax below provides shows you how you can do the same.

```
¹CREATE TABLE CUSTOMER

(

CustID      INTEGER      PRIMARY KEY,

LastName    CHARACTER VARYING (25),

FirstName   CHARACTER VARYING (20),

Address     addr_typ

Phone       CHARACTER VARYING (15) ARRAY [3]

) ;
```

In the above example, the array [3] notation states that you can enter three telephone numbers in the CUSTOMER table in every row. These telephone numbers represent an example of the repeating group. In classical relational database theory, you cannot repeat groups. The arrays are ordered in a way that the element in the array is associated with one ordinal position in this array. Multiset Type

A multiset is not an ordered collection of data, and the elements in a multiset cannot always be referenced. This is because they are not given an ordinal position in the set.

REF Types

REF types are not a part of the actual SQL tool. This means that the DBMS can comply with the latest versions of SQL without the use of the REF type like that. The REF type is not like the CHARACTER and NUMERIC data type, which means that it is not

---

¹ ("Google Groups", 2018)

a distinct data type. It is used as a pointer to a row type, abstract data type or a data item which is in a row in the table. When you dereference a pointer, you can retrieve the value that is stored in the target location. If you want to use the REF type, you should be well-versed with object-oriented programming (OOP).

User Defined Types

The user defined types were another feature introduced in 1999, and these come from the world of object-oriented programming. If you only program using SQL, you are never restricted to the data types that are defined in the later versions of SQL. You can now define your own types by using the principle of abstract data types that are found in object-oriented programming languages.

An important benefit of the UDT is that you can use them to eliminate the impedance mismatch between the host language that uses SQL and SQL. One major problem with SQL is that the predefined data types never match the data types used in the host languages. When you use UDTs, you can create a data type in SQL which will match the data type that is in the host language. The UDT has some methods and attributes. The user can see the method and attributes in a UDT, but the implementation of these methods and attributes will not be shown to the user. You can restrict the access to the methods and attributes by specifying whether they are private, protected or public. Private attributes and methods are only available to the UDT, protected methods and attributes are available to the UDT and its subtype and the public methods and attributes are available to all users. There are two types of UDTs – distinct types and structured types.

Distinct Types

A distinct type is one of the simpler forms of the user-defined data type. The defining feature of this type is that you can express it as one data type only. This type is constructed from a predefined data type which is called the source type. Even if there are many distinct types that come from the same source type, they cannot be compared. For example, you can use a distinct type to differentiate between numerous currencies. Let us consider the following example:

CREATE DISTINCT TYPE USdollar AS DECIMAL (9,2) ;[2]

In the above example, we are creating s new data type for the USdollar variable using the predefined decimal data type. You can create another distinct type in a similar manner.

CREATE DISTINCT TYPE Euro AS DECIMAL (9,2) ;

Let us now create a table that will use these types:

    CREATE TABLE USInvoice (

    InvID   INTEGER   PRIMARY KEY,

    CustID   INTEGER,

    EmpID   INTEGER,

    TotalSale USdollar,

    Tax   USdollar,

    Shipping   USdollar,

---

[2] (TAYLOR, 2010)

GrandTotal USdollar

) ;

CREATE TABLE EuroInvoice

(

InvID   INTEGER   PRIMARY KEY,

CustID   INTEGER,

EmpID   INTEGER,

TotalSale Euro,

Tax   Euro,

Shipping   Euro,

GrandTotal Euro

) ;

The USdollar and Euro types are based on the predefined decimal data type, but you cannot compare the instances of one with another. You can only compare the types once you convert the data into the same currency.

Structured Types

The structured type is another type of the user-defined data type, and this is expressed as a list of methods and attribute definitions that are based on a predefined source data type.

Constructors

The DBME always creates a constructor function when you create a structured user defined data type. This constructor function will have the same name as the user defined type. The function of the constructor is to initialize all the attributes in the structured UDT and declare the values as the default values.

Mutator and observer

If you create a structured UDT, SQL will create an observer function and a mutator function. The latter will change the values of every attribute in the structured UDT while the former will only retrieve the values of the attributes in the structured UDT. You can also user observer functions in a SELECT statement if you want to retrieve values.

Subtypes and supertypes

There can be a hierarchical relationship between two attributes in a structured UDT. For instance, the structured UDT MusicCDudt has two subtypes – RockCDudt and ClassicalCDudt. In this case, the MusicCDudt type if a supertype.

EIGHT

Manage the Objects in Your Database

So far in this guidebook, we have taken some time to look over the data types that you are able to work with inside of your database inside of SQL and we even took some time to look at the commands that you are able to work with to make sure that your queries and more are going to work inside the database. Now we are ready to start learning some of the steps that you need to work with when trying to manage the objects in your database. Some of the different objects that we are going to talk about and which are good to use in the database include synonyms, sequences, clusters, tables, views, and tables. Let's look at some of these examples and learn how you are able to manage some of the different objects that are in your database.

The Schema

When you are working on the schema with your SQL, you should think of it as using a set of objects that are inside the database, but which are linked to just one, instead of all, of the users of the database. This particular user is going to be the owner of the schema, and they get to set the objects, which will be linked back to the username of the owner. For example, anyone, especially the user, will be able to generate the object, and when they do this, they are able to generate their own schemas. This is going to give you some more control over the objects that are in the database, such as the ones that you can change, delete, generate, or manipulate.

This is going to be nice and helpful for people who are trying to use this in order to make some changes to the account. For example, we are going to look at when a new customer is trying to set up an account for your store. This is something that they will sign up for, and they can choose their own password and username that is approved by you, the administrator, of the system. Once the account is set up, they are going to be able to make some changes as is needed, including changing their address, deciding on a new payment option, and even make changes to the items that they are ordering. Any time they want to get into the account, they will just need to use the username and password that they set up, and they can mess around the account as much as they want.

Let's take a little better look at how this will work by bringing out an example. Let's say that you are the person who has the credentials that are needed to login; for this example, we are going to use the username PERSON1. You will be able to decide what you would like to place inside this database and you can even create a brand-new table, for this one we are going to call it EMPLOYEES_TBL. When you then go into the records, you are going to notice that for this new table, it is going to be called PERSON1 EMPLOYEES_TBL; this is how others will see the table name as well, so they know who created the table. The schema is going to be the same for each person who created this table and owns it.

When you would like to access a schema that you own already, you are not required to use the name of the schema; you will simply need to pull it up by its name. So, for the example that we did before, you would just need to call up EMPLOYEES_TBL, but if you would like to pull up a schema from another place, you will need to include the username as well.

Creating a Brand-New Table

When you are creating something in a database, you need to make sure that you are working on tables that will be able to store some of the information that you want. Creating some of these tables is easy, and you will be able to add in the information whenever you need. Whenever you are ready to get started with a brand-new table, you just need to use the command "CREATE TABLE." You can then bring up the table, but there are a few other steps that are needed in order to create this table and make it so that it looks nice and has the right information that you need.

Before you create this new table, you need to consider what you would like to get done with this table, such as how big you would like the table to be, what you would like to put inside and what the organization will be inside. Almost all the SQL types that you are going to use will have characters that you can use if you would like to terminate or submit a statement to the server. A semicolon is a good one to use when working in ORALE but the Transact-SQL version is going to use the GO command. So basically, when you are ready to get started on a table, just type in CREATE TABLE and then fill it all out and you are ready to go.

Creating a new table with one that already exists

There are times when you want to take the information from one table and create a brand-new one. This is possible when you are using the SQL programming; you just need to use the right commands in order to make this happen. The commands that are needed include SELECT and CREATE TABLE. Once you have time to use one of these two commands, you will see that the brand-new table that has the same kind of definitions and parameters as the older table. This is a feature that you are able to make some customizations to so that you can pick what information is going to go from one table to another.

If you would like to take one of your tables and use it to create a brand-new table, you will need to use the following syntax:

CREATE TABLE NEW_TABLE_NAME AS

SELECT ["|COLUMN1, COLUMN2]

Example 1

Let us construct a table to store the information about the weather. You should ensure that you have no repetition in the data. Before you see the answers below, try to write the code.

CREATE TABLE STATION

(ID INTEGER PRIMARY KEY,

CITY CHAR(20),

STATE CHAR(2),

LAT_N REAL,

LONG_W REAL);

Example 2

Let us assume that a table called "Station" is already created. Now, add three rows into this table. This information should be about the train stations in different parts of the United States.

INSERT INTO STATION VALUES (13, 'Phoenix', 'AZ', 33, 112);

INSERT INTO STATION VALUES (44, 'Denver', 'CO', 40, 105);

INSERT INTO STATION VALUES (66, 'Caribou', 'ME', 47, 68);

Exercise

Create a database that contains the information for a computer firm. The database schema should have the following tables:

1. PC (Code, model, speed, RAM, HD, CD, Price)

2. Product (Maker, Model, Type)

3. Printer (Code, Model, Color, Type, Price)

4. Laptop (Code, Model, Speed, RAM, HD, Screen, Price)

The product table provides information about the maker, model number, and the type of product that is available. The model numbers in the product table are unique for all the product types and makers. Every computer is identified by a unique code and is characterized by the model, processor speed, RAM capacity, the hard disk capacity, Speed of the CD Rom, and its price. The laptop table is similar to the PC table except that we use the screen size instead of the CD ROM Speed. For every model in the printer table, its output type, color and printing technology (laser, jet, or matrix) are specified.

NINE

Retrieving Data

What you should be really interested in is the data that is provided to you and not the structure of the database. You want to do four things with data: add it to tables, retrieve and display it, change it, and delete it from tables.

In principle, database manipulation is quite simple. You can always add data to the database or the tables within the database either in a batch or row after row. Deleting, Altering, or retrieving tables are tasks that are easy to perform. The main challenge to database manipulation is selecting the rows that you want to change, delete, or retrieve. Sometimes, retrieving data is like trying to put together a jigsaw puzzle with pieces that are mixed in with pieces from a hundred other puzzles. The data that you want may reside in a database containing a large volume of data that you don't want. Fortunately, if you can specify what you want by using an SQL SELECT statement, the computer does all the searching for you.

Retrieving Data

The data manipulation task that users perform most frequently is retrieving selected information from a database. You may want to retrieve the contents of one row out of thousands in a table. You may want to retrieve all the rows that satisfy a condition or a combination of conditions. You may even want to retrieve all the rows in the table. One particular SQL statement, the SELECT statement, performs all these tasks for you.

The simplest use of the SELECT statement is to retrieve all the data in all the rows of a specified table. To do so, use the following syntax:

SELECT * FROM CUSTOMER ;

The asterisk (*) is a wildcard character that means everything. In this context, the asterisk is a shorthand substitute for a listing of all the column names of the CUSTOMER table. As a result of this statement, all the data in all the rows and columns of the CUSTOMER table appear on-screen.

SELECT statements can be much more complicated than the statement in this example. In fact, some SELECT statements can be so complicated that they're virtually indecipherable. Several modifying clauses can be tacked into a basic statement which gives rise to the potential complexity mentioned earlier. In this chapter, I briefly discuss the WHERE clause, which is the most commonly used method to restrict the rows that a SELECT statement returns.

A SELECT statement with a WHERE clause has the following general form:

SELECT column_list FROM table_name

WHERE condition ;

The column list specifies which columns you want to display. The statement displays only the columns that you list. The FROM clause specifies from which table you want to display columns. The WHERE clause excludes rows that do not satisfy a specified condition. The condition may be simple (for example, WHERE CUSTOMER_STATE = 'NH'), or it may be compound (for example, WHERE CUSTOMER_STATE='NH' AND STATUS='Active').

The following example shows a compound condition inside a SELECT statement:

SELECT FirstName, LastName, Phone FROM CUSTOMER

WHERE State = 'NH'

AND Status = 'Active' ;

This statement returns the names and phone numbers of all active customers living in New Hampshire. The AND keyword means that for a row to qualify for retrieval, that row must meet both conditions: State = 'NH' and Status = 'Active'.

Example 1

Let us retrieve the information in the Table Stations.

SELECT * FROM STATION;

The output will be

ID	CITY	STATE	LAT_N	LONG_W
13	Phoenix	AZ	33	112
44	Denver	CO	40	105
66	Caribou	ME	47	68

Example 2

In this example we will retrieve the information of the stations that are in the North.

SELECT * FROM STATION

WHERE LAT_N > 39.7;

The output will be

ID	CITY	STATE	LAT_N	LONG_W
44	Denver	CO	40	105
66	Caribou	ME	47	68

Example 3

In this example, we will retrieve only the ID, City and State.

SELECT ID, CITY, STATE FROM STATION;

The output will be

ID	CITY	STATE
13	Phoenix	AZ
44	Denver	CO
66	Caribou	ME

Example 4

In this example, we will retrieve the ID, City and State about the stations in the North of the United States.

SELECT ID, CITY, STATE FROM STATION

WHERE LAT_N > 39.7;

The output will be

ID	CITY	STATE
44	Denver	CO
66	Caribou	ME

Exercise

Create a table that stores normalized temperature and information about precipitation. Use the following information to create your table:

1. The ID field should match the ID in Table Station

2. You need to enforce the range for the other values in the table

3. Do not duplicate the Month and ID combinations

4. Temperature should be in Fahrenheit

5. Rainfall should be measured in inches

Once you have created the table, perform the following operations:

1. Populate information for the months of January and July

2. Retrieve all the information in the table

3. Join the two tables

4. Retrieve information about the stations ordering the information by month and greatest rainfall

5. Retrieve information about the temperature in July

6. Query to show the maximum and minimum temperatures

7. Query to convert Fahrenheit to Celsius using a new view

8. Query to show stations with an average temperature greater than 50 degrees

9. Retrieve the data from the new view

The solutions to this exercise are given at the end of this chapter. Before you look at the solutions, try to answer the questions.

Creating Views

The database structure helps to maximize the integrity of data. This is only if you build the database based on some sound principles. The structure is not the best way to look or view the data since different application will use the same data but for a different purpose. They may want to look only at some aspects of the data when they wish to perform some analysis. A powerful feature of SQL is that it can display different views of the data in the database regardless of how the data is stored in the database. The tables that you use to source the rows and columns in a view form the base table. This section will look at how you can use views to retrieve and manipulate data in the database.

You will always receive a virtual table when you use the SELECT statement. A view is a type of virtual table, and each view is different from other views since the metadata in the database holds all the information about a view. This distinction allows you to manipulate a view without having to worry about any other view or the main database. The only issue with using a view is that it is not an independent entity, since it derives its information from the table or tables that you source the information from. Every application can have a unique view of the same data.

Let us look at the following example – a VetLab database contains the following information: CLIENT, TESTS, EMPLOYEE, ORDERS and RESULTS. If the marketing manager or the CEO wanted to understand where the orders are coming from, he will need to pull information from different tables, especially the CLIENT and ORDER tables. If the quality control officer wanted to check what the turn around time for a request was, he will need to source the information from the CLIENT, ORDER and RESULTS tables. They will only need to create a view which will allow them to analyze the necessary information.

Adding Data

A database table is always empty. Once you have created a table using either SQL's DDL or a RAD tool, that table contains nothing but the structured cell. If you want to put the table to use, you will have to add data to it. The data you have may not be stored in digital form.

- If your data is not already in digital form, someone will probably have to enter the data manually, one record at a time. You can also enter data by using optical scanners and voice recognition systems, but the use of such devices for data entry is relatively rare.

- If your data is already in digital form but perhaps not in the format of the database tables that you use, you need to translate the data into the appropriate format and then insert the data into the database.

- If your data is already in digital form and in the correct format, it's ready for transferring to a new database.

Depending on the current form of the data, you may be able to transfer it to your database in one operation, or you may need to enter the data one record at a time. Each data record that you enter corresponds to a single row in a database table.

Adding one row at a time

Most database management systems allow the user to enter data wherever necessary. This feature will allow you to create a form that has a field name. The field labels in the form will give you the chance to determine what type of data can enter the field. The data entry operator will then enter the information into a single row in the form. Once the DBMS accepts that data entered by the user, the form will be cleared which will allow the user to make another entry. This will allow the user to enter one row into the system at a time.

A form-based entry is less susceptible to errors and is easy when compared to using a list which has comma-delimited values. The only problem with a form-based entry is that the values do not have to follow a specific standard. This is because every DBMS has different properties that a user can use when he or she is creating the form. The diversity does not cause an issue with the entry of data. The application developer should always try to understand any change that is made to the form. There are times when some DBMS tools do not allow you to perform some validity checks on the data that a user enters.

The best way to maintain a high level of data integrity in a database is to keep bad data out of the database. When you enter some constraints for different fields, you can prevent the entry of bad or wrong data. This approach enables you to make sure that the database accepts only data values of the correct type and that fall within a predefined range. Applying such constraints can't prevent all possible errors, but it does catch some of them.

If the DBMS tool you are using does not allow you to perform some validity checks on the data, you should build another screen and enter the necessary variables into the screen. You should then check the entries by using any program code. When you are certain that the values entered are correct and valid for every field in the table, you can add more rows by using the SQL INSERT command.

When you want to enter a single row into the database or table, you can use the following syntax:

[3]INSERT INTO table_1 [(column_1, column_2, ..., column_n)] VALUES (value_1, value_2, ..., value_n) ;

You can choose to list the column names in the square brackets ([]). You must remember that the list you provide in the above syntax is the order of the columns that will be in your table. You should put the values in the table in the same order, to ensure that the write values go into the columns. If you want only some values to enter the table, you should list the column name where you want to enter the value. This will tell the tool that a specific value should only be present in that column. If you want to enter a record into a CUSTOMER table, you should use the following syntax: [4]INSERT INTO CUSTOMER

(

CustomerID, FirstName, LastName, Street, City, State, Zip code, Phone

)

VALUES

(:vcustid, 'David', 'Taylor', '235 Nutley Ave.', 'Nutley', 'NJ', '07110', '(201) 555-1963'

) ;

---

[3] (Taylor, 2010)
[4] (Taylor, 2010)

The first value in the table is vcustid which is the primary key. This key will ensure that there is no duplication of data in the table. The value vcustid is entered under the CustomerID column. Since the CustomerID column is the primary key for the full table, the values in this column must always be unique. The remaining columns can contain other data as per the instructions that are provided to the tool. You can also use variables or data types to define these columns if you need to. The INSERT statement works well with both variables or explicit copies of the data as arguments. Deleting Data

New data is being generated every second of every day, and the previous data stored in the database can no longer be of any use. You can remove this data from the database if you want to save space. Old data or useless information will reduce the efficiency of a system. You can transfer old information or data into an archive and place the archive offline. This way, if you ever need to access this data in the future, you can always reload the data from the archive. If you do not want to save the data, you can use the DELETE keyword to remove the data from the system.

If you use an unqualified statement, you can delete all the rows in the table. If you want to delete specific rows in the table, you can use the DELETE and WHERE keywords. The syntax of the DELETE statement is similar to that of the SELECT statement, except that you do not specify the columns in the database. If you delete a row, you will remove all the data in the row.

Let us assume that a customer named David Taylor moved to Tahiti and will no longer purchase any products from you. Therefore, you can remove all the information you have about him from the database.

[5]DELETE FROM CUSTOMER

WHERE FirstName = 'David' AND LastName = 'Taylor' ;

If you have only one customer with the name David Taylor, this statement will delete only that entry. If there is more than one David Taylor in the system, you will need to add the WHERE keyword and include the necessary conditions. These conditions will ensure that you only delete the customer record that you want to remove from the system.

Solutions

1. CREATE TABLE STATS

   (ID INTEGER REFERENCES STATION(ID),

   MOTH INTEGER CHECK (MONTH BETWEEN 1 AND 12),

   TEMP_F REAL CHECK (TEMP_F BETWEEN -80 AND 150),

   RAIN_I REAL CHECK (RAIN_I BETWEEN 0 AND 100),

   PRIMARY KEY (ID, MONTH));

2. INSERT INTO STATS VALUES (13, 1, 57.4, 0.31);

   INSERT INTO STATS VALUES (13, 7, 91.7, 5.15);

   INSERT INTO STATS VALUES (44, 1, 27.3, 0.18);

   INSERT INTO STATS VALUES (44, 7, 74.8, 2.11);

---

[5] (Taylor, 2010)

INSERT INTO STATS VALUES (66, 1, 6.7, 2.10);

INSERT INTO STATS VALUES (66, 7, 65.8, 4.52);

3. SELECT * FROM STATS;

The output will be

ID	MONTH	TEMP_F	RAIN_I
13	1	57.4	.31
13	7	91.7	5.15
44	1	27.3	.18
44	7	74.8	2.11
66	1	6.7	2.1
66	7	65.8	4.52

4. SELECT * FROM STATION, STATS
    WHERE STATION.ID = STATS.ID;

The output will be

ID	CITY	ST	LAT_N	LONG_W	ID	MONTH	TEMP_F	RAIN_I
13	Phoenix	AZ	33	112	13	1	57.4	.31
13	Phoenix	AZ	33	112	13	7	91.7	5.15
44	Denver	CO	40	105	44	1	27.3	.18
44	Denver	CO	40	105	44	7	74.8	2.11
66	Caribou	ME	47	68	66	1	6.7	2.1
66	Caribou	ME	47	68	66	7	65.8	4.52

5. SELECT MONTH, ID, RAIN_I, TEMP_F

FROM STATS

ORDER BY MONTH, RAIN_I DESC;

The output will be

MONTH	ID	RAIN_I	TEMP_F
1	66	2.1	6.7
1	13	.31	57.4
1	44	.18	27.3
7	13	5.15	91.7
7	66	4.52	65.8
7	44	2.11	74.8

6. SELECT LAT_N, CITY, TEMP_F

FROM STATS, STATION

WHERE MONTH = 7

AND STATS.ID = STATION.ID

ORDER BY TEMP_F;

The output will be

LAT_N	CITY	TEMP_F
47	Caribou	65.8
40	Denver	74.8
33	Phoenix	91.7

7. SELECT * FROM STATION
   WHERE 50 < (SELECT AVG(TEMP_F) FROM STATS
   WHERE STATION.ID = STATS.ID);

The output will be

ID	CITY	ST	LAT_N	LONG_W
13	Phoenix	AZ	33	112
44	Denver	CO	40	105

8. CREATE VIEW METRIC_STATS (ID, MONTH, TEMP_C, RAIN_C) AS
SELECT ID,
MONTH,
(TEMP_F - 32) * 5 /9,
RAIN_I * 0.3937
FROM STATS;

9. SELECT * FROM METRIC_STATS;

The output will be

ID	MONTH	TEMP_C	RAIN_C
13	1	14.1111111	.122047
13	7	33.1666667	2.027555
44	1	-2.6111111	.070866
44	7	23.7777778	.830707
66	1	-14.055556	.82677
66	7	18.7777778	1.779524

TEN

Database Security

The users themselves are a major threat to data integrity. There are some users who should never have access to data and there are others who should only have restricted access to the data. You should identify a way to classify the users into different categories to ensure that not every user has the access to classified or privileged information.

If you create the schema, you can specify who the owner is. If you are the owner of the schema, you can decide who you want to grant access to. If you do not grant some privileges, they are withheld by SQL. As the owner of the schema, you can also decide if you want to revoke the access that somebody has to your database. Every user must pass an authentication process before he can access the data he needs to. This process should help you identify the user. That procedure is implementation-dependent.

You can protect the following database objects using SQL:

- Views
- Columns
- Tables

- Character Sets

- Domains

- Translations

- Collations

There are different types of protection that you can use in SQL, and these include adding, seeing, deleting, modifying, using and referencing databases. You can also use different tools that are associated with protecting the queries.

You can give people access using the GRANT statement and remove the access using the REVOKE statement. When you control the use of the SELECT statement, the database tool will control who can view a specific database object like a column, view or table. When you control the use of the INSERT command, you can determine who can enter rows into a table. When you restrict the use of the UPDATE command, you only allow some people to modify the data in the table. The same can be said about the DELETE statement.

If you have a table in the database that has a foreign key which is a primary key in another table, you can add constraints to the first table that refer to the data in the second table. In such a situation, the owner of the first table can extract or analyze the information in the second table. If you, as the owner of the second table, want to prevent the use of your data, you can use the GRANT REFERENCE statement to protect your data. In the following sections, we will discuss the GRANT REFERENCE statement. You will also learn how you can use it to prevent the problem of renegade reference.

Referential Integrity

People believe that their information is protected if you can control who can view, create, modify or delete data. It is true that your database is protected from most threats, but a hacker can still access come confidential information using some indirect methods.

A database has referential integrity if it is designed correctly. This means that the data in one table will always be consistent with the data in another table. Database developers and designers always apply constraints to tables which restrict what data can be entered in the database. If you use databases with referential integrity, users can create new tables that use the foreign key in a confidential table. This will allow them to source information from that table. This column will then serve as the link through which anybody can access confidential information.

Let us assume that you are a Wall Street stock analyst, and many people trust your assessment about which stock will give them the best returns. When you recommend a stock, people will always buy it and this increases the value of the stock. You maintain a database called FOUR_STAR that has the information and all your analyses. The top recommendations are in your newsletter, and you will restrict user access to this table. You will identify a way to ensure that only your subscribers can access this information.

You are vulnerable when anybody other than you creates a table that will use the same name for the stock field as the foreign key. Let us look at the following example.

> [6]CREATE TABLE HOT_STOCKS
>
> (
>
> Stock CHARACTER (30) REFERENCES FOUR_STAR
>
>);

The hacker can insert the name of the stock in the New York Stock Exchange, NASDAQ and American Stock Exchange into that table. These inserts will tell the hacker which stocks he or she entered match the stock that are against your name. It will never take the hacker too long to extract the list of stocks that you own.

You can protect the database from such hacks by using the following statement:

> GRANT REFERENCES (Stock) ON FOUR_STAR TO
> SECRET_HACKER;

You should never grant people privileges if you know that they will misuse them. People never come with a trust certificate, but you would never lend your car to someone you do not trust. The same can be said about giving someone REFERENCE privileges to an important database.

---

[6] (Taylor, 2018)

The previous example explains why it is important that you maintain control of the REFERENCES privilege. The following reasons explain why it is important to use REFERENCES carefully:

- If another user were to specify a constraint in the HOT STOCKS by using the RESTRICT option, the DBMS will not allow you to delete a row from that table. This is because the referential constraint is being violated.

- The first person will need to drop or remove the constraints on a table if you want to use the DROP command to delete your table.

In simple words, it is never a good idea to let someone else define the constraints for your database since this will introduce a security breach. This also means that the user may sometimes get in your way.

Delegating Responsibility

If you want to maintain a secure system, you should restrict the access privilege that you grant to different users. You should also decide which users can access the data. Some people will need to access the data in the database to carry on with their work. If you do not give them the necessary access, they will constantly badger you and ask you to give them some information. Therefore, you should decide how you want to maintain the database security. You can use the WITH GRANT OPTION clause to manage database security. Let us consider the following examples:

GRANT UPDATE

ON RETAIL_PRICE_LIST

TO SALES_MANAGER WITH GRANT OPTION

The statement is similar to the GRANT UPDATE statement that allows the sales manager to update the retail price list. This statement also gives the manager the right to grant any update privileges to people she trusts. If you use this version of the GRANT statement, you should trust the fact that the grantee will use the privilege wisely. You should also trust the fact that the grantee will grant the privilege to only the necessary people.

GRANT ALL PRIVILEGES

ON FOUR_STAR

TO BENEDICT_ARNOLD WITH GRANT OPTION;

You have to be careful when you use statements like the one above. If you misspell the name or give the wrong person access, you cannot guarantee the security of your database.

ELEVEN

How to Work with Search Results Through SQL

O nce you have taken some time to create a brand-new database for your business, there are going to be many times when you need to do a search to find the information that you would like to use. You will be able to use the SQL language in order to find any of the results that you would like, but you need to make sure that the database is set up in the right way for your searches to find your information. Think of it this way; there are times when people will get onto a website that you created, and they are looking for a product that you are selling. Are you more interested in setting up a database that will bring back the wrong results and is slow, or do you want to create a database that is easy to work with and brings back the best results? In this chapter, we are going to take the time to talk about how to get the queries set up right so that your database is going to return the best results.

Creating your New Query

When you are ready to start a new query, you are basically sending out information to the database that is set up. You will need to bring up the right command, the SELECT command, so that you can send out the query that you would like to use. A good example of this is looking at a table that holds all your products inside the database; you will just bring out the SELECT command to find all the products that are in the table. The user, or yourself, will be able to type in the ones that they want to find, such as the best-selling items, ones that are a certain brand, and so on. You can use any kind of query that you would like in order to find the right product from the database.

Using the SELECT command

Any time that you are feeling like creating a query inside the database, you again will need to use the SELECT command for this to happen. This command is going to basically take over starting and executing the queries that you would like to send into the database. In many cases, you just need to add something to the statement, rather than just sending out SELECT, such as the brand of the item that you would like, and then use this command.

Whenever you are using the SELECT command inside of the SQL language, there are going to be four keywords, also known as four clauses, which need to be present. These are going to include:

SELECT

This command will be combined with the FROM command in order to obtain the necessary data in a format that is readable and organized. You will use this to help determine the data that is going to show up. The SELECT clause is going to introduce the columns that you would like to see from the search results, and then you can use the FROM in order to find the exact point that you need.

FROM

The SELECT and FROM commands often go together. It is mandatory because it takes your search from everything in the database, down to just the things that you would like. You will need to have at least one FROM clause for this to work. A good syntax that would use both the SELECT and the FROM properly includes:

SELEC [* | ALL | DISTINCT COLUMN1, COLUMN2]

FROM TABLE1 [, TABLE2];

WHERE

This is what you will use when there are multiple conditions within the clause. For example, it is the element in the query that will display the selective data after the user puts in the information that they want to find. If you are using this feature, the right conditions to have along with it are the AND and OR operators. The syntax that you should use for the WHERE command includes:

SELEC [* | ALL | DISTINCT COLUMN1, COLUMN2]

FROM TABLE1 [, TABLE2];

WHERE [CONDITION1 | EXPRESSION 1]

[AND CONDITION2 | EXPRESSION 2]

ORDER BY

You are able to use this clause in order to arrange the output of your query. The server will be able to decide the order and the format that the different information comes up for the user after they do their basic query. The default for this query is going to be organizing the output going from A to Z, but you can make changes that you would like. The syntax that you can use for this will be the same as the one above, but add the following line at the end:

ORDER BY COLUMN 1 | INTEGER [ASC/DESC]

All of these will need to be in place if you would like to see the SELECT command working properly and pulling out the right information that you are searching for with your query into the database.

Examples

Example 1

Understanding how case sensitivity works

When you are working inside of SQL, you will not need to worry so much about case sensitivity, which is a bit different compared to some of the other coding languages that you will work with. You can choose to use either version of the word, either uppercase or lower case, and it is going to work in your searches. You can even choose to look for statements and clauses if you would like to bring these up.

With that being said, there are several times when case sensitivity is going to be important. One of these times is with objects of data. For the most part, the data that you work with is going to be done in uppercase letters. This is helpful because the other users are going to be able to see that something is consistent inside the code. If you have one user that is typing in JOHN and another who chooses to go with John, people may wonder if they mean the same things or not, so we are going to use upper case to keep everything in order.

Using upper case is one of the best ways to do this because it is easy to read, and you will be used to this from some of the other options of databases that you work with. If you are not using the upper case with your writing, you need to find at least some other method to use that will allow you to remain consistent. If you write out names with the "Name" format, all of them should be this way. This helps others to have an idea of how you are working on different options.

The transactions that you are working with, as well as the queries that go with them, are going to be an integral part of your system and getting it to work out well for you. You may feel that this information is not that important and the user will be able to find all this information whether or not there is a good query that is set up, but if you don't use case sensitivity the right way or make sure that the table is set up the way that it should be, you are going to end up with the wrong results showing up and everyone getting frustrated. No one wants to type words into a query and find out that results that have nothing to do with what they want are coming up.

When you are working on your database, you will need to make sure that the query is set up well so that the customers are able to find the products that they are searching for inside the search bar. When they type in boots, they aren't going to get a bunch of bath toys for example. This is one of the best ways for you to keep customers happy and to avoid a lot of the frustration that comes from not being able to find what they want.

Even if you are not using the database to sell a product, there are going to be times when it still needs to have a good search for the customer. If they want to be able to get some other information from the database, such as their account or a list of the services that you are able to provide, you will still need to have the transaction go as smoothly as possible. Making sure that the database is set up well and that you and the user will be able to find what they want whenever they do a query on your website.

Setting up the queries that you would like to use inside of your database is an important step to making sure that the SQL language is able to find what they are looking for. Whether you are trying to sell products on the site or you would like to make it easy to keep track of all the account information for your customers, you will find that working with making the queries work the right way inside the database can make it so much easier. Use some of the steps that are in this chapter to learn how to set up the database in a manner that makes the most sense and ensures that the right information comes up after your customer does a search.

CHAPTER
TWELVE

An Introduction to Joins

A Structured Query Language (SQL) join is an instruction that you can use to combine the information from two different tables. Before we look at the details of an SQL join, let us look at why you would want to use it. Let us look at two tables that provide information about customers and orders.

Customers

The following table provides information about the customers in a company.

customer_ ID	first_ name	last_ name	email	address	city	State	zip
1	George	Washington	gwashington@usa.gov	3200 Mt Vernon Hwy	Mount Vernon	VA	22121
2	John	Adams	jadams@usa.gov	1250 Hancock St	Quincy	MA	02169

3	Thomas	Jefferson	tjefferson @usa.gov	931 Thomas Jefferson Pkwy	Charlottes ville	VA	22902
4	James	Madison	jmadison@ usa.gov	11350 Constituti on Hwy	Orange	VA	22960
5	James	Monroe	jmonroe@ usa.gov	2050 James Monroe Pkwy	Charlottes ville	VA	22902

The information about every customer is in a separate row. Every column specifies different information including their first name, last name, email ID and State. Every customer is associated with a primary key called the customer_ID.

Orders

order_id	order_date	Amount	customer_id
1	07/04/1776	$234.56	1
2	03/14/1760	$78.50	3
3	05/23/1784	$124.00	2
4	09/03/1790	$65.50	3
5	07/21/1795	$25.50	10
6	11/27/1787	$14.40	9

In this table, every order is associated with a primary key called the order_id. SQL will only look at the order_id when you choose to call upon an order.

How to Use a Join

Let us assume that you want to use the above tables to list all the orders that a specific customer has placed. This can be done by joining or combining the customer and order tables. This can be done by using the customer_id.

> select order_date, order_amount
>
> from customers
>
> join orders
>
>   on customers.customer_id = orders.customer_id
>
> where customer_id = 3

In the above example, we are combining two keywords by using the keyword "join." You should also identify which key (in this example we are using customer_id and order_id) you want SQL to use when you join the tables. This should follow the join statement. The result of this query will be:

order_id	order_date	order_amount
2	3/14/1760	$78.50
4	9/03/1790	$65.50

In this example, we are using the inner join. The method you use is dependent on the type of analysis you want to perform on the data. You can join different tables in multiple ways. In the next section, we will look at left, right, and full joins. The examples in the next sections will use the customer and order tables above.

Basic Types of Join

There are four types of joins – left, right, full, and inner. These joins are different from each other, and the most intuitive and easiest way to explain these differences is by using a Venn diagram. This diagram will show every logical relationship that exists between two tables or datasets.

Before you use a JOIN function on a dataset, you will first need to extract that data and load it into a relational database. These databases will help you to query your data from multiple sources. You can either use an ETL to build the process or build it manually. Let us assume that we have two different data sets – tables A and B. each of these tables have a specific relationship that is defined using a foreign or primary key. The following diagram represents the result of combining the tables together.

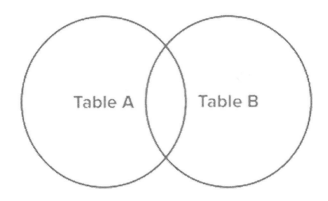

The number of records in Table A that match the records in Table B determine the extent of the overlap in the above diagram. You can use the different types of joins depending on the type of data or the subset you want to select from the two tables.

You can visualize the four types of joins using the following Venn diagrams.

Inner Join

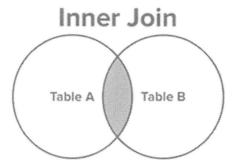

In this type of join, you will select all the records from both tables A and B if and only if the condition is met.

Left Join

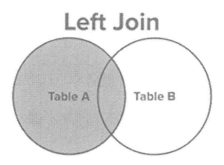

In this type of join, all the records from Table A are selected, and some records from Table B are selected depending on if the join condition is met.

Right Join

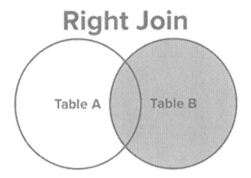

In this type of join, all the records from Table B are selected, and some records from Table A are selected depending on if the join condition is met.

Full Join

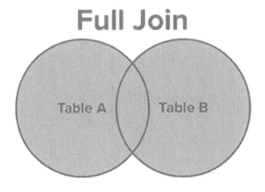

All the records from tables A and B are selected regardless of whether the join condition is met or not.

Examples of SQL Join Types

We will now use the two tables defined at the beginning of this chapter to understand how to use the joins. As mentioned earlier, the relationship between both tables is defined by the primary key, customer_id, in the customer table. This key is a foreign key in the order table.

Customer_id	first_name	last_name	email	address	city	state	Zip code
1	George	Washington	gwashington@usa.gov	3200 Mt Vernon Hwy	Mount Vernon	VA	22121
2	John	Adams	jadams@usa.gov	1250 Hancock St	Quincy	MA	02169
3	Thomas	Jefferson	tjefferson@usa.gov	931 Thomas Jefferson Pkwy	Charlottes ville	VA	22902
4	James	Madison	jmadison@usa.gov	11350 Constitution Hwy	Orange	VA	22960
5	James	Monroe	jmonroe@usa.gov	2050 James Monroe Parkway	Charlottes ville	VA	22902

order_id	order_date	amount	customer_id
1	07/04/1776	$234.56	1
2	03/14/1760	$78.50	3
3	05/23/1784	$124.00	2
4	09/03/1790	$65.50	3
5	07/21/1795	$25.50	10
6	11/27/1787	$14.40	9

You should remember that not every customer in the customer table has placed an order. There are a few orders for which we do not have any customer information in the table above.

Inner Join

Let us assume that we want to extract information from the above tables about the customers who have placed an order. We also want information about the orders placed by that customer. In this case, it would be ideal to use the inner join since this provides information that is common to both datasets.

select first_name, last_name, order_date, order_amount

from customers c

inner join orders o

on c.customer_id = o.customer_id

You will receive the following output:

first_name	last_name	order_date	order_amount
George	Washington	07/4/1776	$234.56
John	Adams	05/23/1784	$124.00
Thomas	Jefferson	03/14/1760	$78.50
Thomas	Jefferson	09/03/1790	$65.50

You should note that John Adams, Thomas Jefferson, and George Washington were the only customers who placed orders. Thomas Jefferson was the only customer who placed two different orders.

Left Join

If you only want to append information about your customers irrespective of whether or not your customer has placed an order, you should use a left join. This join will return all the records in Table A and records from Table B if they match the join condition.

select first_name, last_name, order_date, order_amount

from customers c

left join orders o

on c.customer_id = o.customer_id

first_name	last_name	order_date	order_amount
George	Washington	07/04/1776	$234.56
John	Adams	05/23/1784	$124.00
Thomas	Jefferson	03/14/1760	$78.50
Thomas	Jefferson	09/03/1790	$65.50
James	Madison	NULL	NULL
James	Monroe	NULL	NULL

Since there was no matching record available for James Monroe and James Madison in the orders table, the left join will return a null value. This means that there is no data available for the fields.

You may wonder why this join is useful. If you were to add an extra line of code checking when the order was placed, you will receive the list of customers who have placed an order.

select first_name, last_name, order_date, order_amount

from customers c

left join orders o

on c.customer_id = o.customer_id

where order_date is NULL

Right Join

The right join does exactly the opposite of the left join. This operator will provide information about all the order followed by the information about the customers.

select first_name, last_name, order_date, order_amount

from customers c

right join orders o

on c.customer_id = o.customer_id

first_name	last_name	order_date	order_amount
George	Washington	07/04/1776	$234.56
Thomas	Jefferson	03/14/1760	$78.50
John	Adams	05/23/1784	$124.00
Thomas	Jefferson	09/03/1790	$65.50
NULL	NULL	07/21/1795	$25.50
NULL	NULL	11/27/1787	$14.40

You should note that since there is no matching record for orders placed in the years 1787 and 1795, the name of the customer is null. You should also note the way in which the tables are joined. If you use a right join to map the customer table to the order table, the result would be the same as that of the left join. If you were to add another line to the query "where first_name is NULL," the output will return information about the customers who have placed an order.

select first_name, last_name, order_date, order_amount

from customers c

right join orders o

on c.customer_id = o.customer_id

where first_name is NULL

Full Join

If you want a list of all the records in both tables, you should use the full join.

select first_name, last_name, order_date, order_amount

from customers c

full join orders o

on c.customer_id = o.customer_id

first_name	last_name	order_date	order_amount
George	Washington	07/04/1776	$234.56
Thomas	Jefferson	03/14/1760	$78.50
John	Adams	05/23/1784	$124.00
Thomas	Jefferson	09/03/1790	$65.50
NULL	NULL	07/21/1795	$25.50
NULL	NULL	11/27/1787	$14.40
James	Madison	NULL	NULL
James	Monroe	NULL	NULL

What Do You Do Next?

Using the four types of joins mentioned in this chapter, you can tie up different forms and types of data. This will allow you to ask the right questions and challenge your data. If you have worked on large datasets, you will know that it is difficult to bring the data into a data warehouse or a database, and it is even more difficult to keep the data up to date. This is true if you use different sources to obtain the data. This section talks about how you can integrate all the data from different sources into a data warehouse and learn to maintain the accuracy and quality of data.

It is helpful to work on joins on specific sources or data since it is easier. In most cases, people use data from different sources to perform better analysis. For instance, when you combine marketing data from Facebook or AdWords and the transaction data from your website or account, you can uncover some actionable insights that your company or business can use to maximize profits.

That said, it is difficult to perform joins on data sets that come from different sources. Therefore, you will first need to consolidate the data into a warehouse or database. As mentioned earlier, you can use an ETL service or you can manually extract the data from these sources and consolidate them into a database.

Once the data is in the warehouse or database, you can combine different tables or data from whatever source you want. If you use the Redshift warehouse, you can connect to different business intelligence tools like Wagon, Looker, and Mode. This warehouse also improves the speed of querying. You can view, query, analyze, and visualize the data using reports and charts.

The point here is that it is not easy to use SQL to combine data if you do not store the data in a database or warehouse. The best way to connect to different data sources to obtain data is to use an ETL service like Stitch. Stitch will allow you to connect to different sources that your business uses, and streams all that information into a data warehouse like Redshift. Alternatively, you can stream the data into a database that you have created for the purpose of analysis.

When you have all your data in the warehouse, you can understand how the different sources structure the data. This will help you understand what types of joins you can perform on the dataset.

As mentioned earlier, the data that a company uses to analyze its functions poses a challenge when you wish to use an SQL join. This is because every business uses different sources to obtain the data, and the data from these sources comes in different formats and forms. This makes it difficult to join the data. Therefore, you should use an ETL service since it will make your life easier.

CHAPTER
THIRTEEN

An Introduction to Subqueries

One of the easiest ways to protect the integrity of your data is to avoid any anomalies that may be caused due to any modifications made to the data. You can do this by normalizing your database. In normalization, you will need to break one table into multiple tables using one theme. For example, you should not include product information in the customer table, although the customer has purchased the product.

When you normalize a database or data warehouse correctly, the data will be spread across multiple tables. You will often need to write queries to pull data from more than two tables. You can do this by using the join operators or relational operators (covered in previous chapters). The relational operators will take the information from multiple tables and construct one table. The table will have a different combination of data depending on the operator you are using. An alternative way to pull in data from more than two tables is to use nested queries.

In a nested query, the outermost enclosing statements will contain a subquery within it. This subquery will serve as an enclosing statement for lower-level subqueries that are nested within it. You can have any number of subqueries in the main query, since there is no theoretical limit. It is best to have a limited number of subqueries to avoid implementation difficulties.

A subquery is a SELECT statement, but the outer query can by a SELECT, INSERT, UPDATE, or DELETE statement. A subquery can operate on a table that is different from the table that the outer enclosing statement is operating on. It is for this reason that a nested query will allow you to extract information from different tables.

For instance, if you want to look at the corporate database and list the managers who are older than fifty, you can use joins to obtain this information. The query will be:

SELECT D.Deptno, D.Name, E.Name, E.Age

FROM DEPT D, EMPLOYEE E

WHERE D.ManagerID = E.ID AND E.Age > 50 ;

Here, D is the alias for the Department table, E is the alias for the Employee Table.

The Employee table has a column labeled ID which is the primary key. The ManagerID is the primary key in the department table. This ID is the value of the employee who is the manager of the department. You can use a simple join to pair these tables and the WHERE clause to filter the necessary information. This information will not include the data that does not fit the join criterion. The parameter list includes the DeptNo and Name columns from the Department table and the Name and Age columns from the Employee Table.

Let us assume that you only want the information from the department table while you look at the same rows. This means that you want the information about the managers who are older than fifty, but you do not care who the managers are or what their exact age is. You can use the following subquery instead of using a join:

SELECT D.Deptno, D.Name

FROM DEPT D

WHERE EXISTS (SELECT * FROM EMPLOYEE E

WHERE E.ID = D.ManagerID AND E.Age > 50) ;

This query has the following elements:

1. EXISTS Keyword – one of the many statements used in a subquery.

2. SELECT* in the WHERE clause – this select statement is a subquery.

Why Should You Use A Subquery?

You can use a subquery instead of a join in many instances, and in most cases the complexity of a subquery is the same as the complexity of the join statement. You can decide if you want to use a subquery or a join depending on what you are comfortable with. Most often, people choose to retrieve information from tables using the join operators while others prefer using subqueries. There are times when you cannot use a join statement to obtain the necessary result. In those instances, it would be best to use a subquery. Alternatively, you can break the problem down into multiple statements and execute them one after the other depending on what you need.

What Do Subqueries Do?

A subquery should always be in the enclosing statement and only within the WHERE clause. The function of a subquery is to set the search condition for the WHERE clause. Different subqueries produce different results. Some subqueries produce single values that the enclosing statement used to compare with other values. Other subqueries produce a list of values that the enclosing statement will use as an input. The last type of a subquery returns a Boolean value.

FOURTEEN

An Introduction to Set Operators

You can use a few SQL operators to derive meaningful results from the data in the tables. You can use these operators when you need to use special instructions. This chapter covers the following set operations, with examples:

1. UNION

2. UNION ALL

3. INTERSECT

4. MINUS

UNION and UNION ALL

You can use the union operator in SQL to combine the results that you obtain from two or more queries. These queries are particularly select statements. Before we look at the syntax, there are some points you need to keep in mind:

- The SELECT statements in a UNION should always have the same number of columns

- Every column should have a similar data type

- The columns in every statement should be in the same order

Syntax for UNION

SELECT column_name(s) FROM table1

UNION

SELECT column_name(s) FROM table2;

Syntax for UNION ALL

If you want to include duplicate values when you use the UNION operator, you should include the keyword 'ALL' after UNION. The syntax for this is,

SELECT column_name(s) FROM table1

UNION ALL

SELECT column_name(s) FROM table2;

You must remember that the column names should be the same in the first SELECT statement and the result set.

Sample Database

We will use the Northwind database for this example. Let us look at the sample database from the Customer table.

CustomerID	Customer Name	Contact Name	Address	City	PostalCode	Country
1	Alfreds Futterkiste	Maria Anders	Obere Str. 57	Berlin	12209	Germany
2	Ana Trujillo Emparedados y helados	Ana Trujillo	Avda. de la Constitución 2222	México D.F.	5021	Mexico
3	Antonio Moreno Taquería	Antonio Moreno	Mataderos 2312	México D.F.	5023	Mexico

Let us look at a sample from the supplier's table.

SupplierID	Supplier Name	Contact Name	Address	City	PostalCode	Country
1	Exotic Liquid	Charlotte Cooper	49 Gilbert St.	London	EC1 4SD	UK
2	New Orleans Cajun Delights	Shelley Burke	P.O. Box 78934	New Orleans	70117	USA
3	Grandma Kelly's Homestead	Regina Murphy	707 Oxford Rd.	Ann Arbor	48104	USA

Examples

Example 1

In this example, we want SQL to return the distinct city values from the customers and supplier's tables.

SELECT City FROM Customers

UNION

SELECT City FROM Suppliers

ORDER BY City;

If there is a customer or supplier who is from the same city, the city will only be listed once since the UNION operator only returns distinct values. If you want all the values, you should use the UNION ALL operator.

Example 2

The following example will return all city values including the duplicate values from both tables.

SELECT City FROM Customers

UNION ALL

SELECT City FROM Suppliers

ORDER BY City;

Example 3

In this example, we will use the UNION operator with the WHERE keyword. SQL will return the cities in Germany from both the customer and supplier table.

SELECT City, Country FROM Customers

WHERE Country='Germany'

UNION

SELECT City, Country FROM Suppliers

WHERE Country='Germany'

ORDER BY City;

Example 4

In this example, we will use the UNION ALL operator with WHERE to return all German cities including duplicates.

SELECT City, Country FROM Customers

WHERE Country='Germany'

UNION ALL

SELECT City, Country FROM Suppliers

WHERE Country='Germany'

ORDER BY City;

Example 5

SQL will return all the customers and suppliers in both tables.

SELECT 'Customer' As Type, ContactName, City, Country

FROM Customers

UNION

SELECT 'Supplier', ContactName, City, Country

FROM Suppliers;

Example 6

SELECT product_id FROM order_items

UNION

SELECT product_id FROM inventories;

SELECT location_id FROM locations

UNION ALL

SELECT location_id FROM departments;

Example 7

SELECT location_id, department_name "Department",

  TO_CHAR(NULL) "Warehouse" FROM departments

  UNION

SELECT   location_id,   TO_CHAR(NULL)   "Department",
warehouse_name

FROM warehouses;

Output

LOCATION_ID	Department	Warehouse
1400	IT	
1400		Southlake, Texas
1500	Shipping	
1500		San Francisco
1600		New Jersey
1700	Accounting	
1700	Administration	
1700	Benefits	
1700	Construction	

INTERSECT

The INTERSECT operator will return the result of two or more SELECT statements, but it will only return the rows that SQL selects by all datasets or queries. If there is a record that is present in one result set and not in the other, SQL will not include it in the results.

The Query

The diagram below explains how the clause works. The query will only return the records that are present in the blue shaded area, since these records are present in both result sets. The rules for the INTERSECT clause are the same as the UNION clause.

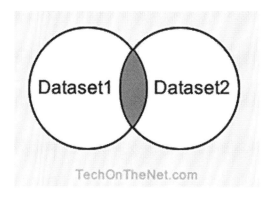

Syntax

The syntax is,

SELECT expression1, expression2, ... expression_n

FROM tables

[WHERE conditions]

INTERSECT

SELECT expression1, expression2, ... expression_n

FROM tables

[WHERE conditions];

Examples

Example 1

In this example, we are using the supplier_id since it will have the same data type in both tables. SQL will return the supplier_id from the order and supplier's table if the ID appears in both result sets.

SELECT supplier_id

FROM suppliers

INTERSECT

SELECT supplier_id

FROM orders;

Example 2

We will continue to use the same example as above, but we will include the WHERE condition to the query. We are including the WHERE clause to both the datasets. SQL will only look at the supplier IDs that are greater than 78 in the first dataset, while it will look at the supplier IDs in the second dataset where the quantity is greater than zero.

SELECT supplier_id

FROM suppliers

WHERE supplier_id > 78

INTERSECT

SELECT supplier_id

FROM orders

WHERE quantity <> 0;

Example 3

Now, let us look at another example where we will see how we can use the INTERSECT operator to return more than one column. The query will return records from the contacts and customer's table if and only if the contact_id, last_name, and first_name match. We are including WHERE conditions in each of the datasets to filter the records where the last_name in the contacts table is not Anderson, and the customer_id in the customer's table is less than 40.

SELECT contact_id, last_name, first_name

FROM contacts

WHERE last_name <> 'Anderson'

INTERSECT

SELECT customer_id, last_name, first_name

FROM customers

WHERE customer_id < 40;

Example 4

In this example we will use an ORDER BY clause with the INTERSECT clause. Since the column names are not the same in the SELECT statements, you can use the ORDER BY clause to refer to the columns in the tables. In the example below, we are sorting through the data in ascending order using the supplier_name and company_name.

SELECT supplier_id, supplier_name

FROM suppliers

WHERE supplier_id > 2000

INTERSECT

SELECT company_id, company_name

FROM companies

WHERE company_id > 1000

ORDER BY 2;

Example 5

SELECT product_id FROM inventories

INTERSECT

SELECT product_id FROM order_items;

MINUS

In this section we will learn more about the MINUS operator. This operator will only return those values in the first SELECT statement that are not present in the second SELECT statement. The SELECT statements define the dataset, and the MINUS operator will retrieve the records from the first dataset and remove the results from the second dataset.

The Query

From the image below, you may have gathered that the MINUS query will return the records that are present in the blue shaded area. These records are only present in the first dataset and not the second. The SELECT statements in the MINUS query should have the same number of fields and similar data types.

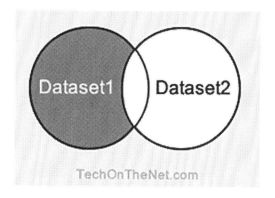

Syntax

The syntax for the minus operator is as follows:

SELECT expression1, expression2, ... expression_n

FROM tables

[WHERE conditions]

MINUS

SELECT expression1, expression2, ... expression_n

FROM tables

[WHERE conditions];

Examples

Example 1

In this example, we will use only one field from both data sets that has the same data type. The MINUS query will retrieve all the supplier_id values which are present only in the supplier's table. This means that if there is a supplier_id that is common to both the datasets or is only present in the second dataset, the MINUS query will not return that supplier_id.

SELECT supplier_id

FROM suppliers

MINUS

SELECT supplier_id

FROM orders;

Example 2

In this example, we will use the ORDER BY clause since there are different column names in both the datasets.

SELECT supplier_id, supplier_name

FROM suppliers

WHERE supplier_id > 2000

MINUS

SELECT company_id, company_name

FROM companies

WHERE company_id > 1000

ORDER BY 2;

Example 3

SELECT product_id FROM inventories

MINUS

SELECT product_id FROM order_items;

CHAPTER
FIFTEEN

Case Study

Most beginners wonder how they can solve problems where they need to combine data from different tables to obtain a single result. The interesting thing is that there are three ways to perform this action, and we have covered them over the course of the book – joins, set operators, and subqueries.

Since this is a comprehensive problem, it is a great idea to use a case study to improve your understanding. If you do not have the SQL Server Management Studio and the Adventure Works 2012 database, you should purchase it now. Most articles online use that version.

Let us now look at the question that was asked.

There is a data table that provides information about different events and there is a series of fields included in this table (reason code, status, and duration). The database also provides information about different statuses. This table has a field that is common to the main table. This allows the user to look at the status and not the code of the event. There are only four statuses that an activity or event can be categorized into – spare, down, ready, and early, and a reason is associated with each status. The reason associated with the status can be the same for more than one event. This source database has four tables for every status where the reasons for the status are stored. Every table has another field which links it to the code for the reason. So, only the status field is missing in the tables.

When you look for something like, when the status in the main table says delay, the query should retrieve the name of the event that has the code for the delay. The query should do the same thing, if the status is down. The query will look for the event in the different status tables.

The goal here is to therefore create a result that does not use codes but uses descriptions. Let us walk through the solution together.

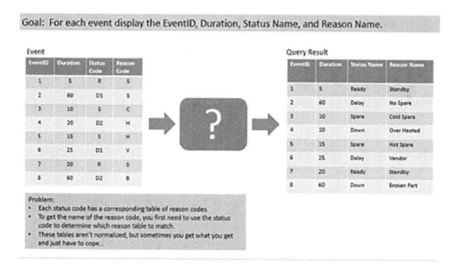

Let us look at the overall view of the different tables and then the problem with matching the tables. In this example, we need to use conditions to math the tables depending on the value of the status.

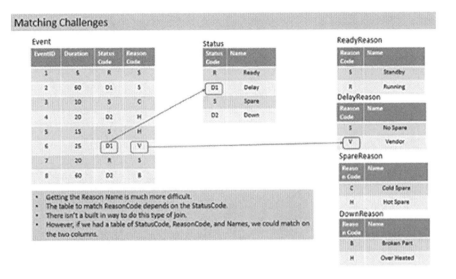

It is easy to derive the status name, and you can use the inner join for this. It is difficult to display the reason name. When you put your mind to it, you will realize that the answer always hinges on how well you understand the different reason tables. If you can treat the reason tables in the same way, you can join them all at once and avoid any duplicate entries which will solve the problem.

If you think about this, you know that you can use a union to perform this function. Every table has the same structure which makes it easier for us to create a derived table. This table will be a result of the combination of the reason tables which can then be joined to the original table using the ready and status code. This will prevent the need to continually match the four tables.

The answer can be broken down into the following solutions:

1. Use a join on the status table to obtain a name.

2. Use a UNION to combine the four reasons tables and avoid the need to use conditional matching

120

3. Incorporate the result in the previous step into the final query using a subquery

Now, let us look at each of these problems in order.

Using INNER JOIN to identify the StatusName

It is important that you obtain the StatusName from the tables that correspond to the status code in the events that you have. For this, we will need to use the INNER JOIN. If you recall, the inner join will return rows only when the join condition is met, and this is the most common join method used. If you remember the examples from the previous chapter, you will know that an inner join can be used to match the primary and foreign keys. Only when these keys match does the query return the rows. This is what you have in the problem. The primary key is the StatusCode in the status table. You should match this code with the StatusCode (foreign key) from the event table. You do not have to worry about the query returning multiple rows since the status code is unique to every record in the status table. Let us look at how this is being done.

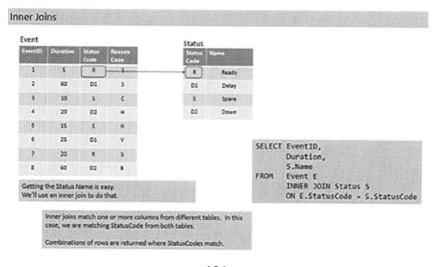

Let u look at the query:

SELECT EventID,

    Duration,

    S.Name

FROM   Event E

    INNER JOIN Status S

    ON E.StatusCode = S.StatusCode

There is more that needs to be done, since you also need to include the reason name. This is however a good start.

Combining Reason Table Rows Using UNION

UNION is one of the different set operators which is a statement used to combine different rows from a table into one result. A join combines columns from different tables into distinct rows for each primary key. The UNION operator adds rows from every table into one table. Let us look at the four separate tables for the reasons.

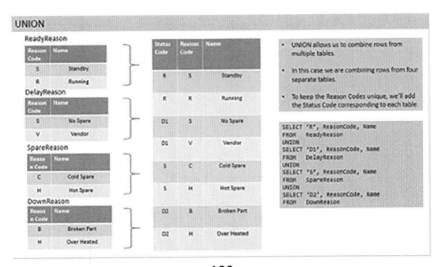

When you apply the union clause, you combine every row from these tables. You will also notice is that you are including a static column which will correspond to the code in the other tables. What I mean by a static column is that it is a fixed value. When you do this, you can associate the rows in every table with a single code. You must remember that this was one of the hurdles that we needed to overcome. We were unable to identify a way to match the records in every table by using a status code. You can use the reason and status codes to match different rows.

```
SELECT 'R', ReasonCode, Name

FROM   ReadyReason

UNION

SELECT 'D1', ReasonCode, Name

FROM   DelayReason

UNION

SELECT 'S', ReasonCode, Name

FROM   SpareReason

UNION

SELECT 'D2', ReasonCode, Name

FROM   DownReason
```

Using a Subquery to Produce the Final Result that Includes the Derived Table

When the union is created, the user can now match that output with the reasons table and match the reasons. The diagram below shows that the matching becomes easier now. You no longer have to look at the status code and map that code to the reason before you can get the name of the reason. You can instead use the standard INNER join and match the derived table with the reason table. You can match the reason code and the status code to identify the reason. You may now wonder how you can include this result in the query.

You can fortunately do this by using subqueries. As mentioned earlier, a subquery is a query that is defined within another query. There are multiple places in a query where you can use a subquery. It is a good idea to use a subquery within a FROM since this statement will refer to derived tables. We now have a derived table which is the result of the UNION. A derived table is enclosed in a parenthesis, but it is also given a name.

UNION in Derived Table (subquery)

If you look closely, you will notice that the UNION result is named SR, and the static fields are assigned a column name. This is to ensure that you refer to the table in the join condition, which makes it easier for a user to read and follow SQL. Let us look at the following code:

```
SELECT EventID,

    Duration,

    SR.ReasonName

FROM   Event E

    INNER JOIN

    (

    SELECT 'R' as StatusCode, ReasonCode, Name

    FROM   ReadyReason

    UNION

    SELECT 'D1', ReasonCode, Name

    FROM   DelayReason

    UNION

    SELECT 'S', ReasonCode, Name

    FROM   SpareReason

    UNION

    SELECT 'D2', ReasonCode, Name
```

FROM DownReason

) SR

ON E.StatusCode = SR.StatusCode AND

E.ReasonCode = SR.ReasonCode

The inner join takes the following form: INNER JOIN {table} ON {match conditions}. In the above example, the derived table replaces the table. It works very well in this case.

Final Query

If you want to create the final result, you need to combine the sub solutions from the sections above. If you look at the solutions from above, you know that what we need to do is relatively simple. The syntax is important to maintain, but the overall idea is straightforward. It can be tough to understand the solution if everything is put together as a query, but I hope you have understood how this solution came about.

Final Query

```
SELECT EventID,
       Duration,
       S.Name as [Status Name],
       SR.Name as [Reason Name]
FROM   Event E
       INNER JOIN Status S
       ON E.StatusCode = S.StatusCode
       INNER JOIN
       (
           SELECT 'R' as StatusCode, 'Ready' as StatusName, ReasonCode, Name
           FROM   ReadyReason
           UNION
           SELECT 'D1', 'Delay', ReasonCode, Name
           FROM   DelayReason
           UNION
           SELECT 'S', 'Spare', ReasonCode, Name
           FROM   SpareReason
           UNION
           SELECT 'D2', 'Down', ReasonCode, Name
           FROM   DownReason
       ) SR
       ON E.StatusCode = SR.StatusCode
       AND E.ReasonCode = SR.ReasonCode
```

Query Result

EventID	Duration	Status Name	Reason Name
1	5	Ready	Standby
2	60	Delay	No Spare
3	10	Spare	Cold Spare
4	20	Down	Over Heated
5	15	Spare	Hot Spare
6	25	Delay	Vendor
7	20	Ready	Standby
8	60	Down	Broken Part

126

```sql
SELECT EventID,
       Duration,
       S.Name as [Status Name],
       SR.ReasonName as [Reason Name]
FROM   Event E
       INNER JOIN Status S
       ON E.StatusCode = S.StatusCode
       INNER JOIN
       (
        SELECT 'R', ReasonCode, Name
        FROM   ReadyReason
        UNION
        SELECT 'D1', ReasonCode, Name
        FROM   DelayReason
        UNION
        SELECT 'S', ReasonCode, Name
        FROM   SpareReason
        UNION
        SELECT 'D2', ReasonCode, Name
```

```
FROM   DownReason

) SR

ON E.StatusCode = SR.StatusCode AND

E.ReasonCode = SR.ReasonCode
```

We can now conclude the case study. I hope you were able to understand the use of joins, operators, and subqueries. When you look at the final query, you can see that it includes the three simple concepts. Most people question the process and how they should write complex programs. This is because they do not know where they can start. You need to remember to progress through the query. This means that you should break the problem down and then try to solve the smaller chunks of the problem before you look at the whole problem.

CHAPTER
SIXTEEN

Ten Rookie Mistakes

Most people often read about SQL only when they are trying to learn how to build relational database systems. You would definitely not study SQL for fun. SQL is used to build applications that function on the database. Before you build one, you will need to either create or extract a database to work on. Several projects often crash far before the code is written on account of an incorrect database. It is imperative that the database that you procure or create has the right structure necessary for the application to work. This chapter covers ten mistakes that are often made when it comes to creating databases.

Assuming your clients know what they need

Clients often call an expert to design and create a database if they have an issue with the current methods being used. They often believe that they have identified both the problem and the solution and all they would need to do is tell you what needs to be done. When you give your clients exactly what they want, you will be digging your own grave. Most managers and users do not possess the knowledge or skills that are necessary to identify a problem accurately. They do not have the skills to identify the solution either.

You will have to convince the client that you have the skills necessary to identify the issues within the system and to analyze the issues within the system you will need to go over the design of the database. The cause is often hidden behind obvious symptoms.

Ignoring the Scope of the Project

When you begin working on developing a new database or an application for that database, you will be told by your client what he or she expects from that application. There are times when the client forgets to tell you something. Over the course of the job, new requirements will crop up, and these will need to be tacked onto the project. Always ensure that everything you are asked to do is delivered in writing before you start working on the project. If you are paid based on a project instead of an hourly basis, these new requirements will definitely turn what was once a profitable job into a huge loss for you. If there are any new additions that crop up, these would need to be compensated for in both time and money.

Considering Technical Factors Alone

Application developers always look at potential projects in terms of whether the project is feasible or not. They will then base their estimates based on that determination. Issues of resource availability, organization politics, cost maximums and schedule requirements always affect the projects. These issues may turn a simple project into a complicated one. Therefore, you must understand the relevant factors before you begin to develop the project. It is always a good idea to decide whether it makes sense to work on the project or not before you begin to work on it.

Never taking feedback

You will always want to listen to your manager because of their experience. The users of any application cannot say much. There are times when you should ignore your manager too, and for a good reason. They often have no idea what the users want , but this does not mean that you know more about the clients and what they need. You should always take feedback from everybody in the organization or team, and only apply that feedback which will help you build a good application.

Using only one Development Environment

You may have spent weeks, months or maybe years to become proficient at using SQL or other database management systems. Regardless of which environment you want to use, you should understand that it has its own strengths and weaknesses. There are times when you need to build an application for which you cannot use the tool you are proficient in , and the best option here would be to bite the bullet. You should tell your clients that the job cannot be done, or you should take some time out to enhance your learning. You can also tell your clients to approach another person or developer for the task if you cannot work on it.

Using one type of System Architecture

The database management systems used in the teleprocessing environment are different from those used in the client and server industry. These systems are also different from the ones that are used in distributed database environments. The databases that you use at work may not always work with other types of data. Therefore, you need to choose the correct architecture even if it means that you pass on the job.

Isolating Database Table Designs

When you identify data objects and the relationships incorrectly, the database table will introduce some errors into the database which will destroy the validity of the results. If you want to design a perfect database, you should always consider the organization of the data in the database, and determine how these data are related to each other. There is no right design that you should use. You only need to determine what the appropriate design is for your data depending on the project needs.

Neglecting Reviews

You should remember that nobody can write the perfect code. Even the best developer may miss some points, and he or she can only identify those points if someone else looks the code. You should always present your work for a review before you release it into the market since that will help you redefine your work. This will help you in improving the program. You should always have a professional review before you begin to develop the code or application.

Skipping Testing

If there is a complex database application that you are using may have some bugs, and it is important that you address these bugs at the earliest. You can test the database in every way possible, but it still may contain some hidden bugs. Therefore, you should give the application to people who do not know what its purpose is, and ask them to use it. They will provide you with more information about the hidden bugs which will allow you to improve your program. You should always learn to fix the problem before it is used by a larger group of people.

No Documentation

If you believe that the application you are using is perfect, and does not have to be adjusted or altered, you need to think again. You must remember that there will come a time when you need to make some changes to the code. You may not remember why you wrote the code in a specific way. Therefore, it is important that you document your work to understand why you wrote the code in a specific way. If you move out of the company or move to a different team, the person who comes in as your replacement should know what needs to be done using the code. He or she should also know why you wrote the code in a specific way. You can always over-document your work since it is important that you add as much detail as you can about the application.

SEVENTEEN

Ten Tips for Easy Retrieval

A database is similar to a virtual treasure of information, and most of this information is hidden from view. You should use the SQL SELECT statement to dig up this hidden information. You may have a clear idea about what information you want to dig up, but it can be difficult to translate that idea into SQL code. If your query is incorrect, you will end up with the wrong results. You should follow the following principles to ensure that your database functions in the appropriate way.

Verify the structure of the database

When you retrieve data from a database and you find that the results are not what you expected, you should check the database design. Many people use poorly designed databases, and you should ensure that you fix your database before you work with it. A good design is necessary to ensure that you maintain data integrity.

Test the Database

You should always create a database which has the same structure as the actual database. This test database does not have to hold all values. You should choose that data for which you know what results to expect. Run the query on the data set and see if you receive the desired output. You may need to reformulate your query depending on the output you need.

You should always build several test data sets that also include some odd cases like extreme values or empty tables. You should always think about the unlikely scenarios and always test for them. You should also look at the proper behavior and make note of it, when you check your database and the queries, you should also understand where you may have issues.

Double Check queries with JOIN

A join is counterintuitive. You must ensure that the JOIN statement in your code is performing in the exact way that you wanted it to. You should add other clauses to the statement only when you are sure that the JOIN statement is working correctly.

JOINs are notorious for being counterintuitive. If your query contains one, make sure that it's doing what you expect before you add WHERE clauses or other complicating factors.

Always check queries with Subselects

Most people misuse the subselect statement. A subselect statement allows you to take the data from one table and use an inner select statement to take the data from another table. You must ensure that the data in the inner SELECT statement is the data that the outer SELECT statement must return as the output. If you have more than one subselect statement, you should be very careful about the code.

Summarize Data using GROUP BY

Let us assume that you have a NATIONAL table that provides information about the PLAYER, TEAM and the number of home runs that the player has scored in the National League. If you want to retrieve the total number of home runs for a team, you should use the following query:

> [7]SELECT Team,
>
> SUM (Homers) FROM NATIONAL
>
> GROUP BY Team ;

This query will list the teams and the numbers of home runs that the team has hit in the season.

Watch out for Clause Restrictions

If you want to use a list of hitters in the national league, you can use the following query:

> SELECT Player, Team, Homers FROM NATIONAL
>
> WHERE Homers >= 20
>
> GROUP BY Team ;

In most database tools, the query will return an error. The columns that you use in a grouping function or in a set function will always appear in the select list. You can use the following syntax for the same:

---

[7] (Taylor, 2018)

SELECT Player, Team, Homers FROM NATIONAL

WHERE Homers >= 20

GROUP BY Team, Player, Homers ;

The query will work in the way you want it to since you want to display all the columns that will appear in the GROUP BY clause. The query will therefore give you the desired results. The SQL tool will first sort the results based on the Team, then by Player and finally by the Homers.

Always Use Parentheses for Logical Operators

When you mix the AND and OR statements in SQL, it will not process the information in the way you want it to. You should always use the parentheses to ensure that you get the desired result. The parentheses also help to ensure that the keywords are applied to the necessary operands or expressions.

Control the Retrieval Privileges

Most people do not use the security features that SQL offers. They do not worry about the security of their data. They believe that only some people will misuse the data in their database. You should never build a database with this mindset. You should always maintain and establish security for any database regardless of its importance.

Create a regular backup

It is difficult to retrieve data if there was a natural calamity like an earthquake, flood or fire. Therefore, you should always create a backup of your data and shift the backup to a safe place. The definition of a safe place is dependent on how critical your data is. You can either save the backup in a room that is fireproof, or in another building depending on what works best for you. You have to ensure that your data is safe and there is a recent backup of the data available for you.

Handle Error Conditions with Grace

Regardless of whether you are embedding queries from an application or into an application or creating an ad hoc query from the console, SQL may return an error message instead of the result. If the error message appears at the console, you can decide what you want to do next based on the error message. If the error message appears in an application, the situation changes since the user is not aware of what action he or she must perform to overcome the error. Therefore, you should always include error handling in your system to cover any error that may arise. It does take time to create an error handling code, but it is always better to include the code instead of staring at the screen when an error message appears.

Additional Tips To Handle Errors

Always use Parentheses

You should always remember to use closing characters to avoid any unbalanced quotes, square brackets, parentheses and double quotes. Experts suggest that you type the open and close characters first before you type whatever data needs to be between the parentheses.

The following error will show you what error you will receive when there are unbalanced parameters:

SELECT lastname, firstname FROM employee

WHERE salary >= (select AVG(salary) from employee ;

ERROR: syntax error at or near ";"

LINE 2: WHERE salary >= (select AVG(salary) from employee ;

Never Use Commas At The End Of Sequences

In SQL, commas act as separators. You must never include a comma between the FROM keyword and the names after the keyword. This is a common error.

SELECT * FROM employee, department,

ERROR: syntax error at or near ","

LINE 1: SELECT * FROM employee, department

Use Partial Query Evaluation To Debug Long Queries

pgAdmin, Navicat and other SQL clients allow you to execute a part of the query. All you need to do is highlight the part of the code you want to evaluate. This way you can fix the code wherever necessary. In the following example, there are two errors.

SELECT llastname, firstname FROM employee

WHERE salary >= (select MAXI(salary) from employee ;

ERROR: column "llastname" does not exist

LINE 1: SELECT llastname, firstname FROM employee

If you execute the complete code, you will get an error about unbalanced parentheses.

SELECT llastname, firstname FROM employee

WHERE salary >= (select MAXI(salary) from employee;

ERROR: syntax error at or near ";"

LINE 2: WHERE salary >= (select MAX(salary) from employee ;

You can also use a subquery and run the program separately. Let us look at the following example:

SELECT llastname, firstname FROM employee

WHERE salary >= (select MAXI(salary) from employee;

ERROR: function maxi(numeric) does not exist

LINE 1: select MAXI(salary) from employee

Pay Attention to Column and Table Names

You must pay close attention to the tab le and column names. Try to paste the names from a previous command since you know that the name will be correct. It is always a good idea to copy and paste the names if you think you cannot type them. If you misspell the name of a table or a column, you should look at the FROM part of your code. You should ensure that the column name is indeed present in the table name that follows the FROM.

SELECT llastname, firstname FROM employees

ERROR: table "employees" does not exist

LÍNEA 1: SELECT llastname, firstname FROM employees

Alternatively, you can use a table name or an alias as the prefix to a column name. This will help when you use two different tables to source the information. The following error will appear if you have identically named columns in different tables.

SELECT lastname, name

FROM department, employee

WHERE depto_id = depto_id

ERROR: column reference "depto_id" is ambiguous

LINE 3: WHERE depto_id = depto_id

SELECT lastname, name

FROM department, employee

WHERE department.depto_id = employee.depto_id

You can fix these errors by including the table name as a prefix to the column name.

CHAPTER
EIGHTEEN

Exercise

This chapter has three tables and a few questions at the end of the chapter. If you are applying to an organization that uses SQL, you should answer the questions in this chapter before you look for the solution at the end of the book.

It is always a good idea to practice questions to master a subject. It is for this reason, that there are a set of thirty questions in this chapter that you can use to improve your learning. You can also use the SQL script in the chapter to create the test data and tables. Most questions in this chapter are those that the top companies and businesses ask.

You will need to use the following tables to answer your queries.

Table 1 - Worker

RKER_ ID	FIRST_ NAME	LAST_ NAME	SALARY	JOINING_ DATE	DEPARTMENT
001	Monika	Arora	100000	2014-02-20 09:00:00	HR

002	Niharika	Verma	80000	2014-06-11 09:00:00	Admin
003	Vishal	Singhal	300000	2014-02-20 09:00:00	HR
004	Amitabh	Singh	500000	2014-02-20 09:00:00	Admin
005	Vivek	Bhati	500000	2014-06-11 09:00:00	Admin
006	Vipul	Diwan	200000	2014-06-11 09:00:00	Account
007	Satish	Kumar	75000	2014-01-20 09:00:00	Account
008	Geetika	Chauhan	90000	2014-04-11 09:00:00	Admin

Table 2 – Bonus

WORKER_REF_ID	BONUS_DATE	BONUS_AMOUNT
1	2016-02-20 00:00:00	5000
2	2016-06-11 00:00:00	3000
3	2016-02-20 00:00:00	4000

1	2016-02-20 00:00:00	4500
2	2016-06-11 00:00:00	3500

Table 3 – Title

WORKER_REF_ID	WORKER_TITLE	AFFECTED_FROM
1	Manager	2016-02-20 00:00:00
2	Executive	2016-06-11 00:00:00
8	Executive	2016-06-11 00:00:00
5	Manager	2016-06-11 00:00:00
4	Asst. Manager	2016-06-11 00:00:00
7	Executive	2016-06-11 00:00:00
6	Lead	2016-06-11 00:00:00
3	Lead	2016-06-11 00:00:00

You need to run the following query if you want to prepare your sample data.

```
CREATE DATABASE ORG;

SHOW DATABASES;

USE ORG;

CREATE TABLE Worker (

        WORKER_ID INT NOT NULL PRIMARY KEY
AUTO_INCREMENT,

        FIRST_NAME CHAR(25),

        LAST_NAME CHAR(25),

        SALARY INT(15),

        JOINING_DATE DATETIME,

        DEPARTMENT CHAR(25)

);


INSERT INTO Worker

        (WORKER_ID, FIRST_NAME, LAST_NAME, SALARY,
JOINING_DATE, DEPARTMENT) VALUES

                (001, 'Monika', 'Arora', 100000, '14-02-20 09.00.00',
'HR'),

                (002, 'Niharika', 'Verma', 80000, '14-06-11 09.00.00',
'Admin'),
```

(003, 'Vishal', 'Singhal', 300000, '14-02-20 09.00.00', 'HR'),

(004, 'Amitabh', 'Singh', 500000, '14-02-20 09.00.00', 'Admin'),

(005, 'Vivek', 'Bhati', 500000, '14-06-11 09.00.00', 'Admin'),

(006, 'Vipul', 'Diwan', 200000, '14-06-11 09.00.00', 'Account'),

(007, 'Satish', 'Kumar', 75000, '14-01-20 09.00.00', 'Account'),

(008, 'Geetika', 'Chauhan', 90000, '14-04-11 09.00.00', 'Admin');

CREATE TABLE Bonus (

WORKER_REF_ID INT,

BONUS_AMOUNT INT(10),

BONUS_DATE DATETIME,

FOREIGN KEY (WORKER_REF_ID)

REFERENCES Worker(WORKER_ID)

ON DELETE CASCADE

);

INSERT INTO Bonus

    (WORKER_REF_ID, BONUS_AMOUNT, BONUS_DATE) VALUES

        (001, 5000, '16-02-20'),

        (002, 3000, '16-06-11'),

        (003, 4000, '16-02-20'),

        (001, 4500, '16-02-20'),

        (002, 3500, '16-06-11');

CREATE TABLE Title (

    WORKER_REF_ID INT,

    WORKER_TITLE CHAR(25),

    AFFECTED_FROM DATETIME,

    FOREIGN KEY (WORKER_REF_ID)

        REFERENCES Worker(WORKER_ID)

  ON DELETE CASCADE

);

INSERT INTO Title

(WORKER_REF_ID, WORKER_TITLE,
AFFECTED_FROM) VALUES

(001, 'Manager', '2016-02-20 00:00:00'),

(002, 'Executive', '2016-06-11 00:00:00'),

(008, 'Executive', '2016-06-11 00:00:00'),

(005, 'Manager', '2016-06-11 00:00:00'),

(004, 'Asst. Manager', '2016-06-11 00:00:00'),

(007, 'Executive', '2016-06-11 00:00:00'),

(006, 'Lead', '2016-06-11 00:00:00'),

(003, 'Lead', '2016-06-11 00:00:00');

You will see the following result on your window:

#	Time	Action	Message
1	21:51:34	CREATE DATABASE ORG	1 row(s) affected
2	21:51:34	SHOW DATABASES	7 row(s) returned
3	21:51:34	USE ORG	0 row(s) affected
4	21:51:34	CREATE TABLE Worker (WORKER_ID INT NOT NULL PRIMARY KEY AUT...	0 row(s) affected
5	21:51:34	INSERT INTO Worker (WORKER_ID, FIRST_NAME, LAST_NAME, SALARY...	8 row(s) affected Records: 8 Duplicates: 0 Warnings: 0
6	21:51:34	CREATE TABLE Bonus (WORKER_REF_ID INT, BONUS_AMOUNT INT(10),...	0 row(s) affected
7	21:51:34	INSERT INTO Bonus (WORKER_REF_ID, BONUS_AMOUNT, BONUS_DAT...	5 row(s) affected Records: 5 Duplicates: 0 Warnings: 0

Once you have the data, you can begin to work on the questions in this chapter.

1. Write An SQL Query To Fetch "FIRST_NAME" From Worker Table Using The Alias Name As <WORKER_NAME>.

2. Write An SQL Query To Fetch "FIRST_NAME" From Worker Table In Upper Case.

3. Write An SQL Query To Fetch Unique Values Of DEPARTMENT From Worker Table.

4. Write An SQL Query To Print First Three Characters Of FIRST_NAME From Worker Table.

5. Write An SQL Query To Find The Position Of The Alphabet ('A') In The First Name Column 'Amitabh' From Worker Table.

6. Write An SQL Query To Print The FIRST_NAME From Worker Table After Removing White Spaces From The Right Side.

7. Write An SQL Query To Print The DEPARTMENT From Worker Table After Removing White Spaces From The Left Side.

8. Write An SQL Query That Fetches The Unique Values Of DEPARTMENT From Worker Table And Prints Its Length.

9. Write An SQL Query To Print The FIRST_NAME From Worker Table After Replacing 'A' With 'A.'

10. Write An SQL Query To Print The FIRST_NAME And LAST_NAME From Worker Table Into A Single Column COMPLETE_NAME. A Space Char Should Separate Them.

11. Write An SQL Query To Print All Worker Details From The Worker Table Order By FIRST_NAME Ascending.

12. Write An SQL Query To Print All Worker Details From The Worker Table Order By FIRST_NAME Ascending And DEPARTMENT Descending.

13. Write An SQL Query To Print Details For Workers With The First Name As "Vipul" And "Satish" From Worker Table.

14. Write An SQL Query To Print Details Of Workers Excluding First Names, "Vipul" And "Satish" From Worker Table.

15. Write An SQL Query To Print Details Of Workers With DEPARTMENT Name As "Admin".

16. Write An SQL Query To Print Details Of The Workers Whose FIRST_NAME Contains 'A'

17. Write An SQL Query To Print Details Of The Workers Whose FIRST_NAME Ends With 'A.'

18. Write An SQL Query To Print Details Of The Workers Whose FIRST_NAME Ends With 'H' And Contains Six Alphabets

19. Write An SQL Query To Print Details Of The Workers Whose SALARY Lies Between 100000 And 500000.

20. Write An SQL Query To Print Details Of The Workers Who Have Joined In Feb'2014.

21. Write An SQL Query To Fetch The Count Of Employees Working In The Department 'Admin.'

22. Write An SQL Query To Fetch Worker Names With Salaries >= 50000 And <= 100000.

23. Write An SQL Query To Fetch The No. Of Workers For Each Department In The Descending Order.

24. Write An SQL Query To Print Details Of The Workers Who Are Also Managers.

25. Write An SQL Query To Fetch Duplicate Records Having Matching Data In Some Fields Of A Table.

26. Write An SQL Query To Show Only Odd Rows From A Table.

27. Write An SQL Query To Show Only Even Rows From A Table.

28. Write An SQL Query To Clone A New Table From Another Table.

29. Write An SQL Query To Fetch Intersecting Records Of Two Tables.

30. Write An SQL Query To Show Records From One Table That Another Table Does Not Have.

CHAPTER
NINETEEN

Using SQL With Applications

We have seen how we can use SQL in isolation. For instance, we went through different ways to create tables and what operations you can perform on those tables to retrieve the required answers. If you only wish to learn how SQL works, you can use this type of learning, but this is not how SQL is used.

The syntax of SQL is close to English, but it is not an easy language to master. Most computer users are not familiar with SQL, and you can assume that there will always be people who do not know how to work with SQL. If a question about a database comes up, a user will never use a SELECT statement to answer that question. Application developers and systems analysts are probably the only people who are comfortable with using SQL. They do not make a career by typing queries into a database to retrieve information. They instead develop applications that write queries.

If you want to perform the same operation continuously, you should ensure that you never have to rebuild that operation from scratch. Instead, write an application to do the job for you. If you use SQL in the application, it will work differently.

SQL in an Application

You may believe that SQL is an incomplete programming language. If you want to use SQL in an application, you must combine SQL with any other procedural language like FORTRAN, Pascal, C, Visual Basic, C++, COBOL, or Java. SQL has some strengths and weaknesses because of how the language is structured. A procedural language that is structured differently will have different strengths and weaknesses. When you combine the two languages, you can overcome the weaknesses of both SQL and the procedural language.

You can build a powerful application when you combine SQL and a procedural language. This application will have a wide range of capabilities. In the discussions in the previous chapters, we use the asterisk to indicate that we want to include all the columns in the table. If this table has many columns, you can save a lot of time by typing the asterisk. It is not a good idea to use the asterisk when you are writing a program in a procedural language. Once you have written the application, you may want to add or delete a column from the table when it is no longer necessary. When you do this, you change the meaning of the asterisk. If you use the asterisk in the application, it may retrieve columns which it thinks it is getting.

This change will not affect the existing program until you need to recompile it to make some change or fix a bug. The effect of the asterisk wildcard will then expand to current columns. This will cause the application to fail when it cannot identify the bug during the debugging process. Therefore, when you build an application, refer to the column names explicitly in the application and avoid using the asterisk.

TWENTY

SQL Embedded Java Program

In this chapter, we will cover information about how you can embed SQL into a Java application. For the purpose of this chapter, we will be using a PostgresSQL database as the backend, but you can use any other database as the backend instead of PostgresSQL. You may need to make some changes to the tutorial. You need to have the following set up on your computer:

1. Java SDK

2. Eclipse DBE

3. Some DBMS

It is very easy to embed SQL into a Java application. You need to use the appropriate JDBC driver in the system for the database. This driver is a file that provides the API that you need to use to write queries in the database. You can use Google to identify which driver you should use for your database. For Postgres users, the driver can be found at the following location: http://jdbc.postgresql.org/. You should download the driver into the directory that you will use for the development of the application.

Once you have downloaded the driver, you can begin setting up the project, and then issue a simple query using the database.

Setting Up a Project in Eclipse

You should first create a new project in eclipse and call it "Database_Tutorial." When the project is set up, you should right click on the project name and select "Build Path" and "Configure Build Path." You should then click on "Add External Jars" and then browse to the JDBC Driver. This will help to set up the environment that will act as the interface between you and your database.

Make the Connection

Now, let us make the connection to the database. You will first need to create a connection object that is surrounded by catch statements. This object will catch those statements that cause some error. The DriveManager.getConnection method will handle the connection that is made to the database. This method also takes the location of the Postgres database, and the name and password that is associated with that instance. Let us assume for this example, that the username is Postgres and the password is pass.

Connection c = null;

```
try {
```

// The second and third arguments are the username and password,

// respectively. They should be whatever is necessary to connect

```
        // to the database.

        c =
DriverManager.getConnection("jdbc:postgresql://localhost/",

        "postgres", "root");
    } catch (Exception e) {


    }
```

You should now try to run the above code in your Java program. If you do not come across any errors, you can be certain that you have connected to the database. Now, you will need to query the database and derive some results that you can play around with.

Let us now perform a simple query on the database. The following code will print the results to the command line.

```
import java.sql.Connection;

import java.sql.DriverManager;

import java.sql.ResultSet;

import java.sql.Statement;

 public class Tutorial {

    public Tutorial(){

        Connection c = null;

        try {

            // The second and third arguments are the username and
password,
```

```java
        // respectively. They should be whatever is necessary to connect
        // to the database.
        c =
DriverManager.getConnection("jdbc:postgresql://localhost/",
            "postgres", "root");


        String query = "Select * From author";
        Statement s = c.createStatement();
        ResultSet queryResult = s.executeQuery(query);


        while(!queryResult.isLast()){


            queryResult.next();
            String authorName = queryResult.getString(1)+",
"+queryResult.getString(2)+", "+queryResult.getString(3);
            System.out.println(authorName);
        }


    } catch (Exception e) {
        e.printStackTrace();
    }
}
```

```
/**
 * @param args
 */
public static void main(String[] args) {
    // TODO Auto-generated method stub


    Tutorial t = new Tutorial();
}


}
```

If you look at the above code, you will see that ResultSet and Statement are two new objects that we have included in the code. These statements allow for the iteration and the execution of the results in the returned rows. The ResultSet object will act as a cursor to the rows returned and that result is looped through every row until the compiler reaches the end of the set.

Adding User Input to Queries

Another way to include user interactivity is to use a Scanner. This Scanner will wait for the first user input and then pass that information along into a method. This method will then build the SQL query and call the database. When you include user input to this program, there is an issue with the threat from SQL injections, which is a hacking tool that most ethical hackers and crackers use.

SQL Injections

An SQL injection is an attack on a website or program which exploits the vulnerabilities in the program. This injection will modify the database which will not produce the desired results. In the LibraryViewer program, an SQL injection can come into any field depending on the input information that someone sends it. Therefore, it is the programmer's responsibility to ensure that he finds a way to minimize this attack.

When you take user input into account, you should avoid the concatenation of the user input and the query.

//BAD!!!

String query = "Select * From author Where authorid ="+id_input;

The above query will take user input. It will then concatenate the input with the query. This is a bad idea since you can either drop or add tables depending on the instructions provided by the user. For example, if the user were to input "1. Drop table books,' the query handler will drop the table books since that is how SQL will read the instruction. To ensure that this does not happen, you should include a type check for every input that the user adds to the query. The compiler should check if the user input is always an integer value.

There is a method called PreparedStatement in Java which makes it difficult for anyone to inject commands into the statement. This is because it parameterizes the SQL query that is being used. The following example has two functions that perform the same task. There is one that uses a prepared statement to ensure that the value is an integer which the other only concatenates that input into the query.

```java
// HELPS PREVENT INJECTIONS BY TYPE CHECKING
AND FORCING PARAMETERIZATION.
public void input(String input){
    Connection c = null;
    try {
        // The second and third arguments are the username and
        password,
        // respectively. They should be whatever is necessary to
        connect
        // to the database.
        c =
DriverManager.getConnection("jdbc:postgresql://localhost/",
            "postgres", "root");


        String query = "Select * From author Where authorid = ?";
        PreparedStatement s = c.prepareStatement(query);
        s.setInt(1,Integer.parseInt(input));
        ResultSet queryResult = s.executeQuery();


        while(!queryResult.isLast()){
```

```
        queryResult.next();

        String authorName = queryResult.getString(1)+",
"+queryResult.getString(2)+", "+queryResult.getString(3);

        System.out.println(authorName);

    }


    } catch (Exception e) {

      e.printStackTrace();

    }


}


// DOES NO SUCH ERROR CHECKING AND JUST CONCATS
THE INPUT STRING TO THE QUERY. VERY BAD!!!
public void inputBad(String input){

    Connection c = null;

    try {

      // The second and third arguments are the username and
password,

      // respectively. They should be whatever is necessary to
connect

      // to the database.
```

```
        c =
DriverManager.getConnection("jdbc:postgresql://localhost/",

        "postgres", "root");


        String query = "Select * From author Where authorid =
"+input+";";
        Statement s = c.createStatement();
        ResultSet queryResult = s.executeQuery(query);


        while(!queryResult.isLast()){


            queryResult.next();
            String authorName = queryResult.getString(1)+",
"+queryResult.getString(2)+", "+queryResult.getString(3);
            System.out.println(authorName);
        }


    } catch (Exception e) {
        e.printStackTrace();
    }
}
```

The PreparedStatement method sets the query up for any values that you want to include in the query. It replaces those values with a question mark. You will see that you have written "Select *" from the author table in the query. This means that compiler will replace every field in the table with a question mark. You can then fill in any missing value by calling the set method. In the above code, we have setInt(1,Integer.parseInt(input)). This method will tell the object that the first variable in the query must always be an integer. A PreparedStatement method is good to cover many types of injections, but there are different ways in which this can happen. Therefore, it is important to remember that you need to have enough tests in your query to get rid of the injections as soon as you can.

CHAPTER
TWENTY-ONE

SQL Embedded C Program

Now, you know how to connect the database to a procedural language, let us write our first SQL program embedded in C. In this example, we will select a station and list all the information for that station. The information for the station comes from the table created in Chapter nine.

```
#include<stdio.h>

#include<string.h>

EXEC SQL BEGIN DECLARE SECTION;


long station_id;

long mon;

float temp;

float rain;

char city_name[21];

long SQLCODE;

EXEC SQL END DECLARE SECTION;
```

```c
main()
{
/* the CONNECT statement, if needed, goes here */
strcpy(city_name,"Denver");
EXEC SQL SELECT ID INTO :station_id
FROM STATION
WHERE CITY = :city_name;
if (SQLCODE == 100)
{
printf("There is no station for city %s\n",city_name);
exit(0);
}
printf("For the city %s, Station ID is
%ld\n",city_name,station_id);
printf("And here is the weather data:\n");
EXEC SQL DECLARE XYZ CURSOR FOR
SELECT MONTH, TEMP_F, RAIN_I
FROM STATS
WHERE ID = :station_id
ORDER BY MONTH;
EXEC SQL OPEN XYZ;
while (SQLCODE != 100) {
```

```
EXEC SQL FETCH XYZ INTO :mon, :temp, :rain;

if (SQLCODE == 100)

printf("end of list\n");

else

printf("month = %ld, temperature = %f, rainfall =
%f\n",mon,temp,rain);

}

EXEC SQL CLOSE XYZ;

exit(0);

}
```

The output will be

For the city Denver, Station ID is 44

And here is the weather data:

month = 1, temperature = 27.299999, rainfall = 0.180000

month = 7, temperature = 74.800003, rainfall = 2.110000

end of list

TWENTY-TWO

SQL Embedded FORTRAN Program

You can also embed SQL in different FORTRAN applications. You will first need to set up the application and enable it to support the use of SQL. The embedded SQL statements in FORTRAN always consist of the following elements.

Correct FORTRAN Element Syntax

Statement initializer

EXEC SQL

Statement string

Any valid SQL statement with blanks as delimiters

Statement terminator

End of source line.

The end of source line is the statement terminator, and if the line is continued, this statement will be the end of the continued line.

Examples of Declaration

1. C Include error handling

    exec sql include sqlca

    exec sql begin declare section

2. C Variables of each data type

byte	dbyte
logical*1	dlog1
logical*2	dlog2
logical*4	dlog4
logical	dlog
integer*2	dint2
integer*4	dint4
integer	dint
real*4	dreal4
real*8	dreal8
real	dreal

    double precision ddoub

    parameter (max = 1000)

    character*12 dbname

    character*12 fname, tname, cname

3. C Structure with a union

   structure /person/

   byte   age

   integer   flags

   union

   map

   character*30 fullnm

   end map

   map

   character*12 first

   character*18 last

   end map

   end union

   end structure

   record /person/ person, ptable(MAX)

4. C From DCLGEN

   exec sql include 'employee.dcl'

5. C Compiled forms

    integer empfrm, dptfrm

exec sql end declare section

    external empfrm, dptfrm

CHAPTER
TWENTY-THREE

SQL Embedded COBOL Program

IDENTIFICATION DIVISION.

PROGRAM-ID. TESTALL.

AUTHOR-NAME. ME.

ENVIRONMENT DIVISION.

CONFIGURATION SECTION.

SOURCE-COMPUTER. IBM-AT.

OBJECT-COMPUTER. IBM-AT.

INPUT-OUTPUT SECTION.

FILE-CONTROL.

DATA DIVISION.

FILE SECTION.

WORKING-STORAGE SECTION.

EXEC SQL

  INCLUDE EMPREC

END-EXEC

01 DISP-RATE PIC $$$,$$$,$$9.99.

01 DISP-COM PIC Z.99.

01 DISP-CODE PIC ----9.

01 FAKE-CHAR PIC X.

01 ANSS PIC X.

01 COM-NULL-IND PIC S9(4) COMP.

EXEC SQL

  INCLUDE SQLCA

END-EXEC

PROCEDURE DIVISION.

172

```
  100-MAIN.

* declare cursor for select

    EXEC SQL

        DECLARE EMPTBL CURSOR FOR

        SELECT *

            FROM EMPLOYEE

        ORDER BY LNAME

    END-EXEC


* open cursor

    EXEC SQL

        OPEN EMPTBL

    END-EXEC

    MOVE SQLCODE TO DISP-CODE

    DISPLAY 'open ' DISP-CODE


* fetch a data item

    EXEC SQL

        FETCH EMPTBL INTO

            :ENO,:LNAME,:FNAME,:STREET,:CITY,

            :ST,:ZIP,:DEPT,:PAYRATE,

            :COM :COM-NULL-IND
```

END-EXEC

100-test.

   MOVE SQLCODE TO DISP-CODE

   DISPLAY 'fetch ' DISP-CODE

* loop until no more data

   PERFORM UNTIL SQLCODE < 0 OR SQLCODE = 100

* display the record

   MOVE PAYRATE TO DISP-RATE

   MOVE COM TO DISP-COM

   DISPLAY 'department ' DEPT

   DISPLAY 'last name ' LNAME

   DISPLAY 'first name ' FNAME

   DISPLAY 'street ' STREET

   DISPLAY 'city ' CITY

   DISPLAY 'state ' ST

   DISPLAY 'zip code ' ZIP

   DISPLAY 'payrate ' DISP-RATE

   IF COM-NULL-IND < 0

     DISPLAY 'commission is null'

```
        ELSE

            DISPLAY 'commission ' DISP-COM

        END-IF

        DISPLAY 'Do you want to see the next record? (y/n)'

        ACCEPT ANSS

        IF ANSS = 'Y' OR 'y'

            EXEC SQL

                FETCH EMPTBL INTO

                    :ENO,:LNAME,:FNAME,:STREET,:CITY,

                    :ST,:ZIP,:DEPT,:PAYRATE,

                    :COM :COM-NULL-IND

            END-EXEC

        ELSE

            GO TO CLOSE-LOOP

        END-IF

        MOVE SQLCODE TO DISP-CODE

        DISPLAY 'fetch ' DISP-CODE

    END-PERFORM .


    DISPLAY 'All records in this table have been selected.'


CLOSE-LOOP.
```

```
* close the cursor

    EXEC SQL

        CLOSE EMPTBL

    END-EXEC


100-EXIT.

    STOP RUN.
```

TWENTY-FOUR

Solutions to Questions
from Chapter Sixteen

This chapter provides the solutions to the questions in chapter sixteen. You must remember that the solutions in this chapter are not the only way to perform the function. You can use an alternative method.

1. Select FIRST_NAME AS WORKER_NAME from Worker;

2. Select upper(FIRST_NAME) from Worker;

3. Select distinct DEPARTMENT from Worker;

4. Select substring(FIRST_NAME,1,3) from Worker;

5. Select INSTR(FIRST_NAME, BINARY'a') from Worker where FIRST_NAME = 'Amitabh';

6. Select RTRIM(FIRST_NAME) from Worker;

7. Select LTRIM(DEPARTMENT) from Worker;

8. Select distinct length(DEPARTMENT) from Worker;

9. Select REPLACE(FIRST_NAME,'a','A') from Worker;

10. Select CONCAT(FIRST_NAME, ' ', LAST_NAME) AS 'COMPLETE_NAME' from Worker;

11. Select * from Worker order by FIRST_NAME asc;

12. Select * from Worker order by FIRST_NAME asc,DEPARTMENT desc;

13. Select * from Worker where FIRST_NAME in ('Vipul','Satish');

14. Select * from Worker where FIRST_NAME not in ('Vipul','Satish');

15. Select * from Worker where DEPARTMENT like 'Admin%';

16. Select * from Worker where FIRST_NAME like '%a%';

17. Select * from Worker where FIRST_NAME like '%a';

18. Select * from Worker where FIRST_NAME like '_____h';

19. Select * from Worker where SALARY between 100000 and 500000;

20. Select * from Worker where year(JOINING_DATE) = 2014 and month(JOINING_DATE) = 2;

21. SELECT COUNT(*) FROM worker WHERE DEPARTMENT = 'Admin';

22. SELECT CONCAT(FIRST_NAME, ' ', LAST_NAME) As Worker_Name, Salary

FROM worker

WHERE WORKER_ID IN

(SELECT WORKER_ID FROM worker

WHERE Salary BETWEEN 50000 AND 100000);

23. SELECT DEPARTMENT, count(WORKER_ID) No_Of_Workers

FROM worker

GROUP BY DEPARTMENT

ORDER BY No_Of_Workers DESC;

24. SELECT DISTINCT W.FIRST_NAME, T.WORKER_TITLE

FROM Worker W

INNER JOIN Title T

ON W.WORKER_ID = T.WORKER_REF_ID

AND T.WORKER_TITLE in ('Manager');

25. SELECT WORKER_TITLE, AFFECTED_FROM, COUNT(*)

FROM Title

GROUP BY WORKER_TITLE, AFFECTED_FROM

HAVING COUNT(*) > 1;

26. SELECT * FROM Worker WHERE MOD (WORKER_ID, 2) <> 0;

27. SELECT * FROM Worker WHERE MOD (WORKER_ID, 2) = 0;

28. SELECT * INTO WorkerClone FROM Worker;

29. (SELECT * FROM Worker)

   INTERSECT

   (SELECT * FROM WorkerClone);

30. SELECT * FROM Worker

   MINUS

   SELECT * FROM Title;

I hope you were able to answer all the questions in this chapter. If you were unable to answer these questions, you should go back to the first few chapters of the book and work on other questions as well. There are tons of questions available on the internet, and there are many tutorial websites that will provide you with different questions that you can practice on.

Conclusion

With this, we have come to the end of this book. I thank you once again for choosing this book.

In today's world, there is a lot of data that is made available to you. If you own a business or want to start a business, you must know how to take care of the data you collect and use that information to improve the functioning of the business. You should also learn to store the information in one location, to ensure that you can access it whenever necessary. Whether you are trying to hold on to the personal information of your customers in one place or you are more interested in putting the sales information in an easy to look at way, you need to have a database that is easy to use.

In this guidebook, we are going to spend some time talking about SQL and how you can use it in a manner that will help you to deal with all your data management needs. SQL is a simple language that can help you analyze your data regardless of the type of business you run. We are going to cover some of the basic information you need to make this system work for you.

There is so much that you can learn about when it comes to SQL and using this system to make your business more successful. This guidebook is going to help you to get started so that you can organize and access your data any time you want to.

Sources

https://www.geeksforgeeks.org/sql-join-set-1-inner-left-right-and-full-joins/

http://www.sql-join.com/sql-join-types

https://www.linkedin.com/pulse/why-should-you-learn-sql-alan-wisniewski-

https://www.systematix.co.uk/sql/12-benefits-of-sql-structured-query-language

https://www.google.co.in/search?q=SQL+exercises&rlz=1C1CHBF_enIN777IN777&oq=SQL+exercises&aqs=chrome..69i57j6 9i59j0j69i60j0j69i60.19388j0j7&sourceid=chrome&ie=UTF-8

http://www.sql-ex.com/learn_exercises.php#answer_ref

https://georgedittmar.wordpress.com/2012/03/02/embedded-sql-tutorial-how-to-write-java-applications-that-need-a-database/

http://www.cs.sfu.ca/CourseCentral/354/zaiane/material/notes/Chapter4/node33.html

http://www.cs.sfu.ca/CourseCentral/354/zaiane/material/notes/Chapter4/node33.html

https://www.ibm.com/support/knowledgecenter/en/SSEPEK_11.0.0
/apsg/src/tpc/db2z_sqlstatementsfortran.html

http://docs.actian.com/ingres/10s/index.html#page/EmbedSQL/Em
bedded_SQL_2fFortran_Declarations_Example.htm

https://www.ibm.com/support/knowledgecenter/SSSNY3_10.1.0/co
m.ibm.db2.luw.apdv.embed.doc/doc/c0006166.html

https://www.essentialsql.com/a-case-study-on-how-to-use-joins-
subqueries-and-unions-to-combine-data-in-sql/

https://www.tutorialspoint.com/sql/sql-operators.htm

https://www.w3resource.com/sql/arithmetic-operators/sql-
arithmetic-operators.php'

https://www.itl.nist.gov/div897/ctg/dm/sql_examples.htm#create%
20view

https://www.dofactory.com/sql/select

https://www.dofactory.com/sql/sample-database

https://www.w3resource.com/sql/arithmetic-operators/sql-
arithmetic-operators.php

Bibliography

1. Google Groups. (2018). Retrieved from https://groups.google.com/d/msg/oracle-plsql/sugqHCyrdPs/ol4Sj8y3IuIJ

2. TAYLOR, A. (2010). *SQL FOR DUMMIES*. [S.l.]: JOHN WILEY & SONS

3. TAYLOR, A. (2010). *SQL FOR DUMMIES*. [S.l.]: JOHN WILEY & SONS

4. TAYLOR, A. (2010). *SQL FOR DUMMIES*. [S.l.]: JOHN WILEY & SONS

5. TAYLOR, A. (2010). *SQL FOR DUMMIES*. [S.l.]: JOHN WILEY & SONS

6. Taylor, A. (2018). How to Ensure Referential Integrity to Protect Your SQL Data - Dummies. Retrieved from https://www.dummies.com/programming/sql/how-to-ensure-referential-integrity-to-protect-your-sql-data/

7. Taylor, A. (2018). How to Ensure Referential Integrity to Protect Your SQL Data - Dummies. Retrieved from https://www.dummies.com/programming/sql/how-to-ensure-referential-integrity-to-protect-your-sql-data/

39745168R00116

Made in the USA
Middletown, DE
19 March 2019